RUSSIA AS EMPIRE

KEES BOTERBLOEM
RUSSIA AS EMPIRE
PAST AND PRESENT

REAKTION BOOKS

Published by Reaktion Books Ltd
Unit 32, Waterside
44–48 Wharf Road
London N1 7UX, UK
www.reaktionbooks.co.uk

First published 2020
Copyright © Kees Boterbloem 2020

All rights reserved

No part of this publication may be reproduced, stored in a retrieval system, or transmitted, in any form or by any means, electronic, mechanical, photocopying, recording or otherwise, without the prior permission of the publishers

Printed and bound in Great Britain by
TJ Books Limited, Padstow, Cornwall

A catalogue record for this book is available from the British Library

ISBN 978 1 78914 291 4

Contents

Preface 7

1 Empire, Imperial Identity and Colonial Rule: The Russian Case 17

2 Empire by Design or Accident of History? 38

3 The Russian Empire in Western Eyes 44

4 Prehistory and Geography: Rus' 59

5 The Mongols, Siberia and Asia 65

6 Moscow's Rise: The Impact of the Byzantine, Polish-Lithuanian and Mongolian Empires on Muscovy 77

7 Troubles 92

8 From Mikhail to Peter: Composite Empire and Middle Ground 101

9 The Waning of the Middle Ground: The Russian, French and British Empires, 1721–1853 121

10 Indirect and Direct Rule: The Russian and British Empires in Asia, 1853–1907 140

11 Multinational Empires: Russia and Austria-Hungary, 1853–1917 156

12 The Soviet Union as Empire, 1917–91 165

13 Since 1991: *Russkii* or *Rossiiskii?* 195

Afterword: Is the Age of Political Empires Over? 206

REFERENCES 210
BIBLIOGRAPHY 226
ACKNOWLEDGEMENTS 233
PHOTO ACKNOWLEDGEMENTS 234
INDEX 235

Preface

This book intends to sketch how the loose confederacy of Kyivan Rus' (*c.* 988–1240) metamorphosed into today's Russian Federation (founded in 1991). In both past and present, Rus'-Russia has been a polity of significant geographic size, in which an Eastern-Slavonic-speaking government ruled, or rules, a great number of varied ethnocultural communities (peoples, *ethnoi*, *narody*). It is, however, a simplistic distortion of the historical process to suggest, as is sometimes done, that a *Russian* empire has uninterruptedly existed in northern Europe and northern Asia for more than a millennium. That for long periods 'Russia' has been an empire is undeniable, but it certainly was not so before 1500, and it is unclear when exactly it did become an empire after 1500. It fell apart several times during the last half millennium as well, returning in a very different form after each collapse. The following, then, investigates what sort of Eastern Slavonic states existed on the Eastern European Plain (and eventually in northern Asia) from the tenth century onward, who its sword-bearers (in a literal and figurative sense) were, and on which ideological pillars these polities may have rested.[1] And it will suggest at which point we could consider these states empires, as well as whether or not we can call today's Russian Federation one. It will ponder the enduring belief in an eternal empire in

Russian collective memory, even if no such everlasting state existed in Russian or Eastern Slavic history.

Russia can be compared both to early modern and modern European overseas empires and to the few longer-lasting empires located within the borders of Europe that existed during the last millennium, such as the Holy Roman and Byzantine empires, the Polish-Lithuanian Commonwealth, or the eighteenth- and nineteenth-century Habsburg monarchy. In some respects and at certain times, it can be compared as well to Asian empires, such as those of early modern India, Iran or China. And in some aspects Imperial Russia resembled its arch enemy, the Ottoman Empire. All of these empires will be occasionally compared or contrasted to the Russian empire, when this is illuminating rather than obfuscating.

The book privileges discussing change over continuity, countering the habit, sometimes open but often surreptitious, of thinking of Russia as some sort of unchangeable empire. Since St Volodymyr's baptism in 988, the political organization of the European and Asian realm that eventually became Russia underwent sweeping transformations. Indeed, as will be explained, the government that ruled Rus' from 988 to approximately 1240 cannot be truly called Russian, despite its confusing name of Rus'. Neither can this Rus' be called an empire. Still, some of the cultural groundwork, particularly in terms of language and religion, was laid in this period to which the subsequent Muscovite, Imperial Russian, Soviet and post-Soviet Russias harkened back.

With the benefit of hindsight, we can discern the first sprouts of a distinctly Russian (as opposed to Eastern Slavic) cultural identity emerge between the mid-thirteenth century and the late fifteenth century; to this era some further origins of a genuinely Russian empire can be traced as well. The development of a Russian language from a common Eastern Slavonic tongue occurs then, while a Russian-Orthodox religion developed that was in several ways different from mainstream Eastern Orthodox Christianity. This happened in a place that was not yet 'Muscovy' or 'Russia', but in what was instead a western borderland of the Mongolian empire. Politically, the principality of Moscow began to surface as the most significant polity under Mongolian rule of this easternmost region of Europe. It wrested itself loose from the Mongol-Tatar embrace towards 1500.

Since about that time a large territory named Muscovy or Russia (and, for three-quarters of a century, the Soviet Union) has been ruled by an independent central government, either from Moscow or from St Petersburg. From approximately 1500 onwards, its leading figures began ever more confidently to consider and style their country an empire, and by about 1700 foreign states and individuals began to accept this claim. This imperial government was composed of people who communicated in Russian, although the sixteenth-century version of this language had a rather different form from that which long-serving Soviet leader Leonid Brezhnev (1906–1982) learned in the early twentieth century, or from the manner in which President Vladimir Putin (b. 1952) speaks today. From about 1547 onwards it became customary for rulers to call themselves *tsar*, or *caesar*, before, from 1721 onwards, calling themselves *imperator*. They then donned the humble moniker of 'general secretary' after the October coup of 1917. Nowadays Russian leaders are titled president, but whether they still preside over an empire is moot.

Whereas its leaders carried the same titles, certain institutions carried the same name, and its elite spoke variations of the same language, the Russian empire of Tsar Ivan IV (1530–1584) was very different from that of Tsar and Emperor Peter the Great (1672–1725), while the latter's empire strongly differed from that of Emperor Alexander II (r. 1855–81). Even its capital was not always the same city. The post-1917 Soviet Union shared few features with its predecessors, while the post-1991 Russian Federation is very unlike its predecessor, despite lazy or facile equations of the two in public discourse.

The chasm between each of these 'Russias' (and the sometimes utterly swift transformation of the country) reminds one in some ways of Michel Foucault's scheme to divide history into some sort of epistemically defined periods, each phase being totally different from the others, and separated by 'ruptures', as the French thinker proposed in *The Order of Things* (*Les mots et les choses*).[2] Whereas in each of these epochs the same words were sometimes used in depicting some aspect of the workings of a Russian empire, those words signified something very different for each of those completely different polities. In some ways, Philip Longworth adopted a version of this analysis in his interpretation of Russian history by identifying four distinct imperial Russias in history: those of Kiev (Kyiv), of Riurikid Muscovy, of the Romanovs, and of the Soviet era.[3] The transition phase between these periods was dramatic, indeed in many ways revolutionary: the Mongol invasions; the Time of Troubles; the 1917 revolutions; and the implosion of 1991 can all be read as radical ruptures of the Foucauldian type.

I largely agree with Longworth's idea of the existence of five significant Russian states in history that are each quite different, but I apply another chronology and use different terms.[4] Furthermore, the principality of Kyiv (*c.* 950–*c.* 1230), despite its large nominal size, was neither an empire nor Russian, nor

Ukrainian, for that matter.[5] I differ from Longworth as well by suggesting that another 'rupture' might be identified in Peter the Great's reign, while I am not convinced that the Time of Troubles, despite its intense mayhem, represents a true watershed.[6] Meanwhile, a quarter millennium of Mongol-Tatar rule cannot be ignored, as he does, as a historical phase, even if no 'Russia' is clearly identifiable or distinct from the Mongolian empire in this period.

So my 'imperial' chronology is Kyivan Rus', Mongolian interlude, early modern Muscovy, Imperial Russia, Soviet Union, and Russian Federation, with only Imperial Russia and the Soviet Union being true and independent empires. There are hints at an imperial identity throughout early modern Muscovy (*c.* 1480–*c.* 1700), but this identity was not always clearly articulated and often seems more the reflection of wishful thinking than of reality. In this, Muscovy resembles today's Russian Federation somewhat. The radical turning points are Christianization, Mongol subjugation, liberation from Mongol rule, Peter's reign, the 1917 revolution and the 1991 collapse.

I agree with Longworth that what we call Russia meant something very different in various historical periods, both to Western observers and to those who lived in the various iterations of this empire.[7] In other words, the cliché that 'Russians like to be ruled by dictators', which sees certain wits crudely link Mongol khans with Ivan IV, Peter, Catherine, Nicholas I and II, Lenin, Stalin and Putin, is as meaningless and untrue as to say that the British are inveterate monarchists, ignoring the vast difference between the power and status of William I and Elizabeth II, the numerous royal dynasties ruling England, the Cromwellian intermezzo, or the different historical paths of Scotland, Northern Ireland and Wales.

The first chapter discussing what 'empire' means in the Russian context is followed by a short chapter looking at how much the development of such an empire was willed, brought into being purposefully, and briefly addressing the question of whether or not mere historical accident or a measure of deliberate planning (a loaded word in the Soviet context) informed the creation of the post-1500 empires. Chapter Three intends to dismiss some of the more pernicious myths about 'the Russian empire' and its expansionism that have been current in the Western world ever since the sixteenth century. Chapter Four's portrayal of the pre-Muscovite history of Russia, Belarus and Ukraine should disabuse the reader of any notions about an eternal Russian empire that has existed since primordial times. This cannot be done without some assessment of the role of geography and of how scholars have suggested it influenced the course of history in this part of the world, because of the undeniably exceptional challenges it presents to human habitation.

During the first half-millennium of their history, the Eastern Slavs were not politically organized in an independent empire ruled by a Slavic monarch. Nonetheless, the Slavs in theory and sometimes in practice were subject to an emperor. During the first half of this era, this was the Byzantine emperor, who closely collaborated with Constantinople's Orthodox patriarch (and the Church was rather more influential in Rus' than the *basileios*). As Chapter Five shows, when the collapse of the Byzantine empire before the Fourth Crusade in the early thirteenth century made Rus' lose its Byzantine overlord, he was soon replaced by descendants of Chingis Khan (1162–1227). Both Byzantine and Mongolian heritage left an imprint on Muscovite political culture, although it is a matter of debate how deep each stamp was and when, and to what extent, it faded. Because of the gradual drift of the western parts of Rus' towards the orbit of the Polish kingdom and the Lithuanian principality, the historical path of the Eastern Slavs began to differentiate by the mid-fourteenth century. This led to the development of three distinct languages and cultures, with all the consequences that followed, up to and including the events of 2014.

After looking at Rus' and the Mongolian era, we turn in Chapter Six to independent Muscovy, first led by the last Riurikids (among whom especially Ivan III and Ivan IV are noteworthy) who attempted to establish a new Orthodox empire to replace the definitively defunct Byzantine polity after 1453 and concomitantly claim the succession to the western khanates of the Chingisids. This dual direction of Muscovite policy was not very clearly conceived or consistently pursued; regardless, it had the outcome of a composite empire with a diverse population in terms of religion, culture and language. Ivan IV further confused matters by coveting territories west of Muscovy inhabited by Western Christians (even if he did not gain much in this direction).

Although Ivan IV cannot be wholly absolved from responsibility for the chaos that befell his empire soon after his death, the Time of Troubles (*c.* 1598–1613), outlined in Chapter Seven, was probably mainly caused by the succession crisis after the death of his son Fyodor I (r. 1584–98) and the extreme conditions that worsened Russia's already harsh climate heading into the seventeenth century, which triggered a cascade of failed harvests, famine and epidemic diseases. Remarkably, under a different dynasty the devastation of the Troubles was relatively quickly overcome and much of the territory of Ivan

IV's composite empire was recovered by the Romanov regime within a few years after 1613. As the subsequent chapters show, the first Romanovs not only consolidated in Europe but oversaw an eastward expansion that in short order added Siberia to Muscovy's possessions. This came at a high price: the harnessing of much of the population to serve the empire as enserfed peasants, producing food for the warriors serving the tsar.

As important as the Siberian expansion was the first stage of the Russian absorption of Ukraine. It began in the 1650s, prompted more than anything by religious motives. Different from his father and grandfather, Peter the Great consciously made his country into a European monarchy (returning in this respect to the days of Kyivan Rus' half a millennium earlier), and tried to shake off much of the obsolete and non-European aspects of Russian political culture. When officially proclaimed emperor by 'his grateful subjects' in 1721, Peter set in motion a two hundred-year period in which Russia was very much a key player among Europe's five Great Powers. His successors (especially Catherine II) gained more territory in Europe, but also moved deeper into Asia, eventually joining the Great Game with Britain in the borderlands of Turkestan, Afghanistan and India. Many of especially these eighteenth- and nineteenth-century acquisitions spelled trouble down the road, and were lost in the conflagration of the First World War and Civil War. Some were recovered by the Soviet Union during the early 1920s, some others by 1945. In 1991, all these territories gained their independence, and Russia was almost reduced to the territory Muscovy had encompassed at the accession of Aleksei Mikhailovich in 1645.

The limits of Russia's imperial power became evident in the Crimean War. Towards 1900, Russia clearly began to suffer from

Preface

what Paul Kennedy has called 'imperial overstretch'.[8] Checked by the British in Middle Asia, the Russians almost seemed to try to re-enact Chingis's conquests in the opposite direction. China may have seemed ripe for the taking, but Japan (and Britain) were not going to let the Russians have their way in East Asia. Russian eastward expansion thus stalled in 1905 as well. Chapter Eleven ponders what might have become of Imperial Russia if it had not been destroyed in the First World War; for most of the twentieth century, historiography held that Russia and Austria-Hungary were empires doomed to collapse under the weight of rising nationalism, regardless of the outbreak of war in 1914. If so, however, the Communists could hardly have put the Soviet Union together from the shards of the post-1917 Russian empire.

The last two chapters address the resurrection of the Russian empire in its new guise as the Soviet Union, and its dismantling. In 1919, there were at least two governments claiming to be the legitimate successors of the tsar's regime. The rump that clustered around Moscow and St Petersburg proved more durable. By 1921 many formerly tsarist territories had been added to this rump, Bolshevik Russia, while its competitors withdrew from the field. The Soviet Union gained force (at astounding human cost) for the next two decades and then proved strong enough to withstand Hitler's marauders (at equally astounding human cost). Although the war bled the Soviet Union white, the country that emerged from it after 1945 was even larger than the tsarist empire of Nicholas I. Indeed, a number of countries on the other side of the official Soviet border fell under Moscow's control as well, and remained so until 1989. Again, the collapse was swift: first, in the autumn of 1989, those satellites left the Soviet Bloc, and then, in the summer of 1991, the Soviet Union itself fell apart into fifteen independent states, the Russian Federation being one of them.

Putin's Russia is still geographically a large state, and it has more nuclear weapons than any other country on earth, bar the United States. But despite its grandiose posturing, and the sometimes panicky Western response to its moves, it is not at all clear whether today's Russia is an empire, and it is equally dubious whether it can be, or even wants to be, an empire again.

1
Empire, Imperial Identity and Colonial Rule: The Russian Case

What is an empire? As Krishan Kumar reminds us, the concept of empire, at least as understood in the European world, is rooted in the Roman Empire of antiquity.[1] But it came to mean different things in different places at the close of Europe's classical age, when the idea of a universal realm ruled by one monarch was contested. Western and Eastern Roman empires took shape, of which the first had disappeared by 500.[2] The surviving Eastern Roman Empire is usually known as the Byzantine Empire, named after Byzantium, the original name of its capital, Constantinople, situated along the waterway separating Europe from Asia. This empire was Greek rather than Roman in its language and culture. During the tenth century, the Eastern Slavs were converted to Christianity by Byzantine missionaries, clerics who adhered to the Greek Orthodox iteration of Christianity. Still today, the Russian and Ukrainian Orthodox churches consider themselves subordinate to the first patriarch of Orthodoxy, who resides in Istanbul (the Turkish name for Constantinople).

But the Byzantine Empire was also important in another way for the history of the Russian empires. The grand prince of Muscovy donned the mantle of the Byzantine emperor after the fall of Constantinople to the Ottoman sultan's armies in 1453. Significantly, the nomenclature for the Russian

The Soviet Union in the 20th century.

(Muscovite) monarch derived by way of Byzantium from the classical Romans' usage of the word *caesar* (originally a mere last name) as one of the titles for their emperor: *tsar*. The Slavonic-speaking Bulgarians, for a while the great enemies of the Byzantines, had adopted this title in the tenth century, but Russian usage of the title came into vogue much later, only after the fall of Constantinople. Before that the highest ruler among the Eastern Slavs was called the grand prince (*velikii kniaz*, sometimes rendered as 'grand duke' in English), which suggested that he was at least nominally subordinate to a higher-placed monarch, the Byzantine emperor. In adopting the title of tsar, the Russians inherited the Byzantine challenge to the Western claims to universal monarchy of the *kaiser*, the 'Holy' Roman emperor, whose German title equally derived from the Latin *caesar*.

Claiming to rule as emperor and exerting absolute power are not necessarily complementary. The Roman emperors of antiquity had in theory enjoyed far-reaching powers because they combined the role of secular ruler (and supreme military commander) with that of their state's religious head as high priest (*pontifex maximus*). A vestige of previously enjoyed religious supremacy stuck to the emperor even after Christianity became the state religion in the course of the fourth century. But like every allegedly all-powerful ruler before the arrival of modern technology, the exercise of imperial power was severely hampered by the lack of sophisticated means of transport and communication. His hold being tenuous, the emperor had to concede significant authority to others, not least in his proconsuls and satraps of remote regions, to avoid rebellions and the like. Routinely, Roman emperors went on campaign to defeat enemies within and without their empire, thereby underlining their ability as military commanders. But permanent campaigning was not an option for logistical and economic reasons. The emperor entrusted deputies with ruling peripheral areas. The stability of this construction was facilitated because the *pax romana* benefited most imperial subjects, providing peace and prosperity rather than the violent anarchy that (was thought to be) common in many of the territories beyond the *limes*.

Although no longer considered a semi-divine figure, the Christian Byzantine emperor maintained an aura that made him seem more than a mere human being, and his advocates in their written and spoken rhetoric made him into an autocrat (from the Greek words *autos* and *kratein*), a single ruler with supreme power who was God's infallible representative on earth. His awesome might was depicted for eternity on the religious buildings of Constantinople and elsewhere, juxtaposed to imposing images of Christ and God as the creator and ruler of all (or *pantokrator*).[3] As long as the emperor's armies succeeded in defending the realm, and as long as there were no disputes about the succession to the throne, few dared to challenge his rule. To a degree, we can trace the overbearing deference Russian subjects harboured for their tsar in word and deed to this exalted status of the Byzantine emperor. The Russian Orthodox Church, especially, cultivated the tsar's semi-divine status in its rhetoric, both in orally delivered sermons and in its writings. After 1500, for the great majority of the Russian population, the tsar became a *batiushka*, the little lord on earth, the deputy who did the bidding of the great lord in heaven. Once he fell from this pedestal and began to be criticized as a mere mortal, which happened ever more strongly after 1850, his authority rapidly dwindled.

Previously, however, Muscovites grovelled before their tsar, calling themselves for example in written petitions his slaves and giving themselves demeaning diminutive names ('sweet tsar, your little servant Vanya [that is, Jacky, who was actually Prince Ivan Mikhailovich Miloslavskii], humbly beseeches you to come to his aid'), while they practised their own version of kowtowing in ceremonial encounters with the tsar. Peter the Great changed some of these overly self-diminishing rituals, but paradoxically did introduce some newfangled imperial routines that echoed the Roman Empire, having his senate call him *imperator* in 1721; even earlier, after a successful campaign against the Tatars at Azov, he had passed in a Roman-style triumphal march through a temporarily raised imperial arch in Moscow.[4] Until the Decembrist Revolt of 1825, at least, public deference to the tsars and tsarinas after Peter was hardly less marked than before he took the reins from his half-sister Sophia in 1689. Lenin (V. I. Ulyanov, 1870–1924) and Stalin (I. V. Dzhugashvili, 1878–1953) enjoyed their own 'cult of personality' that made them larger than life, while Vladimir Putin (b. 1952), too, seems to have recaptured this sort of semi-divine status, at least in the eyes of some of his voters (in which, again, the Russian Orthodox Church plays a role).

Russia's latter-day leaders ruled, and rule, empires encompassing a hundred or more ethnic groups and nine time zones. Without arguing for a direct link between the enormous size of the territory they ruled and the almost unlimited power they (at least in theory) enjoyed over their subjects, it does not seem wholly coincidental to many that, in what has now been for centuries the largest country in the world, the government resembles more of an autocracy than a democracy in which checks and balances limit the power of the ruler. How truly unlimited the power was – or is – of the Russian tsars, Soviet dictators or Russian president is moot, but many continue to believe that Russia coheres best if it is at least formally ruled by a powerful leader unencumbered by too many restraints. All experiments with shared governance, the argument goes, have been brief and occurred when Russia was at its weakest as a Great Power.

This is then quickly linked to the Putin era. As in the Roman empire in its heyday, Russia's (alleged) current peace and prosperity go a long way in explaining the Russian acquiescence to a government that hardly anyone ever holds accountable for its deeds. If anyone doubts this, a comparison with the equally passive Kazakhstan of Nursultan Nazarbaev (b. 1940) can be held up as illuminating. People acquiesce in an authoritarian leader's rule as long as wars are won and borders defended, while being left to a considerable degree to their own devices in search of prosperity and welfare. But this line of argument is a little bit too simple, and leads back to the caricature many people elsewhere cherish about the Russians and their political predilections.

What is rather more persuasive is to suggest that democracy is everywhere a recent experiment, and the term 'democracy' means different things in different places (indeed, as one of my teachers stressed, there is no such thing as an ideal democracy, just an ongoing process of democratization, or its reversal). The experience of an 'imperial presidency' in the USA has challenged the idea of the separation of powers. The insignificant degree to which a U.S. president can be held accountable for his deeds challenges the idea of the U.S. being a democracy as such, especially when presidents are elected by an electoral college rather than the majority of voters, while much of the electorate does not even bother to vote. In Russia, democracy has not made much headway in the direction of a true system of checks and balances, in which the population feels that it has agency. The period 1905–14 presents perhaps a brief spell of such progress, together with a few months in 1917. From about 1990, voters regained a somewhat meaningful choice at the ballot box in Russia, but that choice more or less disappeared by the time Vladimir Putin was re-elected in 2004. That does not mean that we may not see a renewed wave of democratization in the near future in Russia.

While one may question the authenticity of the public or ostentatious worship of an all-mighty ruler, it should be noted that enough Russians (and we do have to use this term, as it applies to early modern Muscovy (1462–1721), Imperial Russia (1721–1905), the Soviet Union (1917–91), and the Russian Federation (since 1999)) have considered themselves stakeholders in the Russian imperial projects to defend its existence, just as many people in the USA support their country even if it is ruled by an imperial presidency.[5]

'Russia', of course, meant something different at different times to its inhabitants, but, at least since the fifteenth century, time and again a common identity of sorts has been forged, shared by a sufficient number of people who intend to preserve a Russian motherland (*rodina*) or fatherland (*otechestvo*): Russians are somewhat unique in using both terms to refer to their native land. Despite all the mysticism and the esoteric character of much of his writing, the philosopher Nikolai Berdyaev (1874–1948) astutely perceived the existence of a Russian version of the American Manifest Destiny, or even a Russian identification with the Old Testamentical Chosen People.[6] This idea can be traced to those faraway days of

Constantinople's fall and the Muscovite defiance of their Mongolian overlords in the second half of the fifteenth century. The concept of Russia as a nation is not merely based on an invented tradition or imagined community forged in the nineteenth and twentieth centuries, as has been the case in many countries around the world.[7] The current Russian idea goes back further. And the Russian people constitute a nation that derives its identity in part from having been the torch-bearers of an empire for more than half a millennium.

Meanwhile, I have not yet clearly suggested what empires are and what sort(s) of empire Russia has been. I will use a fairly loose and straightforward definition here: *empires are geographically large polities, whose political authority usually encompasses many ethnic groups, who speak a variety of tongues*, even if often one administrative language is used, such as Latin, Ottoman Turkish, Han Chinese, Urdu or Russian. It is difficult to say when a state is too small to qualify as an empire, and there is no consensus among academics regarding certain polities: for example, the Netherlands and Belgium had substantial overseas colonies by 1914, but both were rather small – and militarily weak – states within Europe. I suggest that they should hardly be considered empires, despite their overseas territories.

A short foray into languages other than English provides some additional food for thought. Different languages use different words to describe empires: for Dutch speakers, for example, the word *rijk* (akin to the German *Reich*) means the government administration as well as the polity of the mainland Netherlands and its overseas territories (which today have been reduced to a few islands in the Caribbean), whereas a state ruled by an emperor (*keizer*, from caesar) is called by the composite term *keizerrijk*, as opposed to a *koninkrijk*, which is a monarchy ruled by a king (*koning*) or queen (*koningin*). More precise terms such as these would be useful in English, which uses a word derived from Latin to connotate empire. It is telling that the English government was probably the first Western polity that equated the title of tsar in Russia with that of emperor, and began to address the Muscovite monarch as such as early as in the reign of Queen Elizabeth I (1558–1603).

In the Russian language, various words are used to describe the realm of the tsar and the land of the Soviets, or indeed today's Russia, which is usually called the Russian Federation even if it is in fact quite centralized, something that the word 'federation' challenges. Thus one finds *Rossiiskaia Imperiia*, or its predecessor *Russkoe*, or *Rossiiskoe, tsarstvo'*, which was self-consciously adopted by Ivan IV (1530–1584) at his official coronation in 1547.[8] It was his grandfather Ivan III (r. 1462–1505) who began to use the term 'tsar', to claim succession to the last Byzantine emperor whose niece he married. But there are other words in Russian connotating a large state, such as *prostrantstvo* ('expanse') or even *vselennaia* ('universe', or 'world').

The Russians may have acquired an us-versus-them mentality early on, likely in some part because of their embattled existence as subjects of the Tatar khans. Such things are reflected in the language. Today, too, one often encounters the *nash* ('us') versus *ne nash* ('not us') dichotomy by which Russians approach alleged, imagined or real others. As in many other cultures, such as Imperial China, which considered itself the Middle Kingdom around which other polities orbited as satellites, the world was Russia, and Russia was the world, as expressed in the word *mir*, meaning at the same time 'village' and 'world'. Visitors from the West were, for example, called *nemtsy*, from singular *nemets* or 'mute', or 'he, who cannot speak'. This was not just a country, but a world, from the moment it began to define itself in its early modern form, around 1500. A similarly solipsistic worldview can be seen in the Russian word for Orthodox Christian believer, *pravoslavnyi*, which originally meant something along the lines of 'right believer', suggesting that everyone else was wrong – even if this is a word that is not exclusive to Russian but shared with other Slavic languages. Because their land was surrounded by enemies, a sort of collective bunker mentality spilled into the Russians' language. Even in the seventeenth century, Western visitors still witnessed villagers fleeing when catching sight of foreigners, or hiding their wives and children. And the elite sequestered their women in the so-called *terem*, a Byzantine habit. Only under Peter the Great did Russian noblewomen begin to appear in public.

This exclusivity was paired with an inclusiveness that is intriguing and *sui generis*.[9] For the Russians have been comparatively welcoming to other peoples who joined their empire. One of the secrets of the longevity of Russia has been the country's significant willingness to allow others to become part of it. The roots of this tolerance are difficult to pinpoint. It seems appropriate here to ponder the importance of a third key influence on the Russian concept of empire and Russian imperial behaviour, that of the Mongols.[10] Despite their fearsome reputation, the Mongols fairly early enlisted Turkic warriors into their armies, and proved tolerant of their subjects as long as tribute was paid and resistance was shunned.[11] Moscow adopted this accommodating attitude, one reason why it became the leading Rus' principality under Mongol rule, and why it expanded its size.

It is germane here to ponder the suggestion by Vasily Kliuchevskii (1841–1911), the greatest pre-1917 Russian historian, that the medieval settlement of Slavonic crop cultivators among Finno-Ugrian hunter-gatherers in what is now Central and Northern (European) Russia was a largely peaceful process of ethnic mixing.[12] The surviving sources, however, are too few and one-sided (that is, written by Slavonic speakers) to truly prove this; but, whether in emulation of Mongol (Tatar) practice or following the pattern of their previous settlement among the Finno-Ugrian communities, in later times the Russian authorities unhesitatingly co-opted foreign princes and their retainers into their own elite, while they often agreed to treaties with non-Russians that promised to leave the latter's culture inviolate.[13] These promises were often kept for centuries, and until well into the nineteenth century Russian administrators or Orthodox clergy were quite circumspect in dealing with many of the non-Russian subjects of the tsar. The 'friendship of the peoples' (*druzhba narodov*) principle of the Soviet Union (even if based on a different theory about the organization of human life) appears an echo of this custom. This explains perhaps too why extremist ethnic nationalism does not have much traction in today's Russia, and is only reluctantly harnessed by Putin's government: too many of its own members are of mixed ancestry, and some of the best-known public figures have no ethnic Russian ancestors at all.[14] And, likewise, too many of Putin's supporters are of diverse ancestry.

Whereas after 1500 many members of the elite among the Cherkess, Kazakhs, Ruthenians, Poles or Baltic Germans preferred to reside in their homelands and stay away from Moscow or St Petersburg, those who did move to the capital needed to master the Russian language. Eventually, they, or their

The Solovetsky Monastery on an island in the White Sea was converted into an early Gulag camp from 1923 to 1939.

descendants, became acculturated and more Russian than anything else.

A tension might develop between permitting local communities' autonomy and the practical needs and requirements of the central government, however, which could not always be resolved without conflict. Until 1916, Central Asians were spared conscription because it did not seem worth the trouble of offending cultural sensibilities by having Kazakhs, Tajiks or Uzbeks undergo basic military training under the lead of largely Christian-Slavic instructors. In the desperate shortage of manpower in the First World War, however, the Muslims of Turkestan were called up for the army, with disastrous consequences. Most seemed to have ignored the mobilization order, while some revolted in what is called the Basmachi Rebellion, a conflict that lasted until the middle of the 1920s (and the Soviets inherited from the tsar). It proved the previously prevailing wisdom of the Russian government of leaving people as much as possible to their own devices.

This live-and-let-live mindset, then, suggests that Russia in its earlier guises, before the Soviet Union was founded, was a composite empire in the way H. G. Koenigsberger and J. H. Elliott described most larger early modern states.[15] Recently, a fine case study by Matthew Romaniello underlines how that concept is applicable to early modern Muscovy.[16] In other words, different parts were ruled according to different sets of rules, rather than everyone falling under the same uniform law code. Still, in 1649 the tsar and his closest allies did try to impose a set of basic laws that were universally applicable across Russia (and this was not the first of its kind). This *Ulozhenie*, though, was an incomplete document that did not codify anything regarding many important aspects that structured the complex non-Russian societies in late Muscovy, or their relationship with the Russians.[17] Dealing with such legislative lacunae was left to the discretion of local administrators, who before Peter's reign were usually military governors (*voevody*) assisted by a few clerks (*d'iaki*) and a garrison of musketeers (*strel'tsy*) or Cossacks. Although receiving decrees from the tsar's government in Moscow, these proconsuls seem to have largely abided by the treaties concluded with the local peoples. Wary of having them become too entrenched in their region, these Russian satraps were frequently rotated by the tsar to stop them from developing intimate entanglements with the local population.

Both sides, as Mikhail Khodarkovsky has argued, understood the so-called *sherty* agreements and similar treaties in their own way, with the Russians usually interpreting the terms as testimony to the native population's submission, while the latter read them as a reflection of an alliance of equal partners.[18] The most notorious example of this sort of mutual misunderstanding may be the 1654 Treaty of Pereiaslavl' between the Ukrainian chief Bohdan Khmel'nits'kii (1595–1657) and Tsar Aleksei Mikhailovich (1629–1676).

Ukraine's autonomy was gradually curtailed, with Catherine the Great (1729–1796) naming some of the annexed lands previously ruled by Tatars and Poles 'New Russia', rather than incorporating them into Ruthenia, Ukraine's more traditional name. The empress ignored the indigenous Ukrainian inhabitants of her southern territories in her invitation to German farmers to settle and develop ostensibly uninhabited land. The government's more imperious behaviour in this instance (when compared to the earlier circumspection of the *sherty* or even 1654) may reflect the transition to a more modern empire. Only in the nineteenth century did a sustained, albeit slow, process begin that reduced the autonomy of non-Russians in earnest. This concerted drive was significantly aided by the compilation of the Russian laws undertaken by Mikhail Speranskii (1772–1839), a much more comprehensive codex than the *Ulozhenie*, that was completed in 1832. Speranskii had been for many years Siberia's governor and was sensitive to the relationship between Russians and the multitude of non-Russian communities living there. In his compilation, most of the legislation governing the relationship between Russians and non-Russians was included, unlike its spotty coverage in the 1649 code.

Although almost concomitant with this reduction of particularistic rights and privileges, the first stirrings of modern nationalist movements were not necessarily a response to this 'Russification'. For instance, Ukrainian nationalism was inspired, too, by the rising European nationalist movements, while Polish nationalist revolts (even if they grew substantially in the course of the century) broke out even when the Poles enjoyed an autonomy that was far greater than that of almost any other ethnocultural group in the tsar's empire.

And the drive to implement a uniform set of rules and regulations applying to all the tsar's subjects remained cautious, even when it was undertaken. Even such a momentous decree as that which abolished serfdom in 1861 did not equally apply to all parts of the empire; and while the time at which peasants gained their freedom might vary according to their location within the Russian empire, the manner by which they were released (with or without land, and so on) from the bonds to their lords varied as well. Tsar Alexander II's other 'great reforms' of the 1860s and '70s were similarly calibrated to the specifics that distinguished the many territories that composed his realm. Thus military conscription was not universally introduced, nor were the bodies of local self-government, the *zemstva*, introduced outside most of the non-Slavic areas. And in the second half of the nineteenth century the Russian authorities in the newly conquered lands in Central Asia (then often called Turkestan) were very cautious in establishing their administration, leaving the population alone for the most part, and ignoring the Russification policies on which they embarked elsewhere. Only the major towns in this region were staffed with Russian bureaucrats and patrolled by Slavic soldiers. Few attempts were undertaken to develop this vast area economically, despite boasts that the Russians had ended the local slave trade and brought civilization in other forms. No one dared to undertake any campaigns to convert the Muslim inhabitants to Orthodoxy, while almost everything else of the local traditions was left unperturbed.

This was the closest the Russians came to a version of the indirect rule practised by the British in some parts of India. This type of soft (or almost friendly) colonialism might be linked to the rise of a decidedly peaceful intellectual movement that called for a modernization of Islam, that of Jadidism. It believed in a happy marriage between modernity and Muslim tradition and seemed for a long time more influential than any inveterate hostility to the imposition of Russian rule as expressed in extremist Muslim movements. Of course, the Russians needed to tread carefully: the 1916 enlistment of Muslim men under infidel command in the Russian army proved too crude a step for many and led to a violent reaction.

Interestingly enough, the Soviet Union, in theory, also began as a sort of composite empire.[19] And even after its establishment in 1924, the Communists' state was composed of equal parts (eventually fifteen socialist soviet republics). This was no longer going to be a 'prisonhouse of nations', as tsarist Russia had been according to the revolutionaries, but a state led by the principle of the friendship of its peoples.[20] In practice, however, something very different obtained: the USSR was centralized to the hilt, with every key decision rendered by a small bunch of men residing in Moscow. It was during the three-quarters of a century of communist rule in Eastern Europe and Northern Asia that a truly heinous form of colonial domination prevailed, albeit strangely punctured by overtures towards indigenous self-determination and celebrations of local culture. The outcome of these contradictory policies, after 1991, has been mixed. Some of the smaller ethnicities have been exterminated (at least in a cultural sense, and even at times in a literal sense) by the Soviet experiment, but many others have found a more coherent collective voice than ever before. Here the soft-line policy of the support for local languages and cultures in the Soviet republics (Ukraine, Belarus, Georgia, Uzbekistan and so on) and even in the 'autonomous' regions (Tatarstan, Bashkiria, Kalmykia, Chechnya), combined with a brutal regime of persecution and privileging of Russians, or sometimes of all Eastern Slavs, has led to a strongly felt national identity among a majority of people.[21] In its turn, this mass nationalism among non-Russians has triggered, or strengthened, mass nationalism among the Russians. Its origins go back a long way, as I argued earlier, but through various jolts it became a mass phenomenon, from the introduction of general conscription in 1874, to the spread of mass literacy, the Russification policies of Alexander III and Nicholas II, urbanization and industrialization, the culturally Russian nature of the Soviet Communist party, and Stalin's and his successors' propagating of the advanced (or superior) nature of the Russian nation, considered first among equals (at a minimum) in the Soviet Union.

Russian nationalism today is sustained by a bunker mentality, rooted in a sense that the non-Russian republics unjustifiably single out the Russians rather than the Soviet Union as the cause of all their sufferings, on the one hand, but, on the other hand, also from the conviction that the West and the countries of the 'near abroad' gang up on them in an attempt to subjugate Russia and keep it down. With Russia's economic fortune drastically improving after 2000 came a sort of superior taunting of the successor states, and offers of economic advantages in exchange for the renewed acceptance of Russian political leadership. Not only can the Russian Federation as such, then, be seen as a Russian state in which millions of non-Russians are bossed around by Russians (or have to pass as Russians in order to truly belong), but it is clearly involved in establishing a sort of economic dominance along its perimeter, even if this latter effort may have only been truly successful in Belarus.[22] But whether or not Russia today is a full-fledged empire remains a matter of opinion.

The widespread Russian support for the increasingly aggressive foreign policy of the Putin era is also due to a phenomenon not entirely unfamiliar in the motherlands of other former empires: imperial nostalgia. The self-worth of many Russians was rooted in their sense of being denizens of a vast and powerful empire (indeed, a superpower) without whose consent little of consequence could happen in the world. On the road to this dominance, many sacrifices were made, not least the bloodshed that hallmarked the Stalin era. Too many facile or one-sided explanations have been made about the psychological attraction of being an imperial subject, but, no doubt, many feel great pride in belonging to a powerful country.[23]

A different but related question is whether or not the population benefited, or benefits, from being part of an empire. On the one hand, as with the *pax romana*, it can be argued that the Russian empire provided a more orderly form of existence within its borders than existed outside of it. Indeed, for various periods prosperity was great enough to lead to a remarkably sustained population growth, as occurred in Russia during the eighteenth and nineteenth centuries. Here, though, the puzzle is whether or not this growth came about because of or despite the protection and stability the empire provided. Across Europe (and even globally) the eighteenth century witnessed a steady population growth, as did the nineteenth. This seems to have been the result of a somewhat milder climate (especially after 1750) and an absence of major epidemics. Additionally, in the nineteenth century, certain improvements in health care, especially inoculation against various contagious infantile diseases and a better sense of hygiene surrounding childbirth, curbed mortality. One might suggest that the empire deserves credit, but even then many of the inoculation drives were spurred on by local initiative, not least by those who worked for the *zemstva* after 1870. The Russian empire's death rate by 1900, though, still far outstripped that of industrialized Europe. And the Soviet era did nothing much to improve people's lives, certainly not before 1953. Of course, some did experience real improvements in gaining access to technical and cultural amenities, especially if they moved to the cities from a countryside bereft of water provisioning, sewers and electricity, and where education was at best basic, but one has to weigh such improvements against the suffering of those in the civil war, subsequent famine, dekulakization, another famine, the Great Terror, countless extra deaths during the Second World War as a result of the poor preparation or readiness of the country, and the post-war famine and further purges.

Living during the heyday of European imperialism in the later nineteenth century, Kliuchevskii, again, suggested that the European overseas and overland empires of his era were essentially similar colonial empires.[24] In this he was right, probably, even if the genesis of the Russian empire was very different from that of the British or French. Debate still rages among historians as to whether or not any tangible benefit derived from empire for the mother country (for which the term *metropolis* is often used). Lenin thought so, suggesting that the Western working class owed its relatively high standard of living to colonial exploitation. Others suggest that the benefits were far less apparent, if one balances the costs of the colonial armies, the navy, the training and payment of colonial officials, or the construction of roads, bridges, schools, hospitals, telegraphs and telephones against the benefits of the markets found for the mother country's exports, the raw materials extracted to be processed in the factories and workshops of the metropolis, and so on. Certainly, empire made the fortune of many a European individual exploiting its opportunities. But there was a reason the Western Europeans quickly abandoned their colonies after the Second World War: they cost far more than they yielded. Relieved from their imperial burden, the standard of living in Europe reached unprecedented heights.

The Soviets had a chance to abandon the tsarist colonies in the early 1920s, but for ideological reasons (and possibly out of military considerations as well) they more or less restored the Russian overland colonial empire Kliuchevskii identified. Although there are a number of reasons why the Soviet experiment failed, the cost of developing and militarily defending the non-European parts of the country (Siberia perhaps excepted) was a significant contributing factor. Long after the European colonial empires had been dismantled, the Soviets held on to theirs, at great expense and to the detriment of the standard of living of the Russians, Ukrainians and Belarusians.[25]

2

Empire by Design or Accident of History?

The British Empire, it has sometimes been said, was created as an afterthought: the overseas territories fell into the hands of the English (and Scots) almost by accident, as their prime interest was in overseas trade. To help this commerce along, colonies were established. But it was not as easy as that: for instance, the fighting in, and occupation of, Ireland, the travels of indentured servants or religious exiles who populated British North America in the seventeenth century, the transportation of Africans to the Caribbean and of convicts to Australia show the strained effort and sometimes outright malice involved in triggering British expansion, belying the idea of a bunch of carefree spirits with a knack for business founding an accidental empire. If so disinterested in territorial acquisitions, indeed, why did the British not return Québec to France in 1763, or Ceylon and South Africa to the Dutch in 1815?

Still, for a long time the British Empire was hardly driven by any grand imperial strategy beyond an effort to dominate the world's overseas trade routes. Overseas territories accumulated somewhat randomly and were apparently even lost (as in the case of the United States) without too many regrets. In similar fashion, Russia, too, won and sometimes lost territories without much of a design behind conquering or keeping them.

Empire by Design or Accident of History?

Thus Peter the Great, after several previous Russian attempts had failed to bridle this region, managed to conquer the Tatar stronghold of Azov in the mid-1690s, which was a considerable feat that came at a high price. But he gave up on this fortress within two decades to wrest himself out of a war with Ottoman Turkey that threatened to become a true fiasco (oddly enough, Peter's reputation as a great military commander and political leader did not suffer from this disaster).[1] After successfully forcing the Swedes to concede the St Petersburg area and parts of today's Estonia and Latvia, Peter also launched a successful campaign to conquer the southern shore of the Caspian Sea, which had been part of Safavid Iran. Once the Iranians recovered from their domestic turmoil, however, the Russians gave up this rather large territory without much of a fight in 1732. It seems as if in the eyes of the Empress Anna Ioannovna (r. 1730–40) and her advisors this possibly strategic outpost was not worth the trouble to keep it. While northern Iran for a short while was a sort of Russian-Soviet protectorate in the early twentieth century, no serious attempt had been taken in the intervening two centuries to reoccupy the territory Peter had gained there.

Therefore, contrary to Richard Pipes's (and many others') argument that Russia has historically shown a voracious, incessant and insatiable appetite to expand, and desperately held on to every inch of territory it conquered, Russia did abandon expansionist efforts on a number of occasions.[2] Usually this was done because the cost was seen as far outweighing the benefit, especially if maintaining a foothold meant deploying substantial armed forces: see, too, the Russian acceptance and adherence to the 1689 Treaty of Nerchinsk with Qing China (only in the late 1850s did the Russians feel strong enough to challenge its terms), or the 1867 sale of Alaska to the United States. And Tsar Alexander II very reluctantly accepted the conquest of vast swaths of Inner Asia, where some of his generals had gone on a rampage heading punitive expeditions that sought to end border incursions into Russian territory by various gangs hailing from Turkestan. The tsar made sure that the Russian expansion across the Caspian Sea did not provoke Britain into another conflict, a mere few years after the end of the Crimean War in 1856. Russians were not always enthusiastic conquerors, in other words, which a study of the long-drawn-out acquisition of Poland or the Caucasus shows as well.

No doubt the strategic decisions of the tsars and tsarinas were at times informed by the desire to have easier-to-defend natural borders, if such seemed feasible (seas such as the Black and Baltic Seas and the Pacific Ocean, or mountain ranges such as the Caucasus or Urals), but this goal was often trumped by other aims, of which the desire for an ice-free port is the best known. Indeed, Arnold Toynbee (1889–1975) suggested in his still thought-provoking, albeit often factually mistaken, essay 'Russia's Byzantine Heritage' that Russia's wars had almost always been defensive, whether Novgorod's against the Swedes and Teutonic knights in the thirteenth century, or those of Muscovy against Tatars and Poland-Lithuania in the fifteenth and sixteenth centuries, against Poland and Sweden in the early seventeenth century, Napoléon in 1812, or Hitler in the Second World War.[3] The country's expansion was mainly the result of an effort to acquire borders located as far as possible away from the Russian heartland around Moscow and the Novgorod area. Toynbee (as so many did before 1991) left unexplained how the gradual absorption of Ukraine or Siberia fits into this defensive strategy, but it can be argued that the Muscovites in those regions preempted the conquest by another imperial rival, such as the Uzbeks or Qing (Siberia), or a resurgent Ottoman Empire (Ukraine).[4]

AFTER 1917, A clear imperialist blueprint is again hard to discern, this despite the fact that the desire to determine precisely the contours of the Soviet empire's economic development through planning became a sort of fetish. The State Planning Bureau (*Gosplan*) mapped out in excruciating detail the optimal production levels of the country's industry and, to a significant degree, agriculture, but plan fulfilment rather occurred on paper than in reality in almost all economic sectors.[5] Commodity distribution and transportation were likewise carefully laid out, but goods and services were in actual fact poorly supplied. Personal initiative was heavily circumscribed.

Oddly, though, this minute planning was not matched by the designing of any grand blueprint of the future Soviet Union, despite some very general slogans about the 'radiant future', or the Marxian 'withering away of the state'.[6] It was not spelled out in how far the Soviet Union was to either expand or join in a sort of confederation with other countries, once they were ruled by Communist governments. Nor was it explained how exactly within the Soviet Union a true communist society would emerge, after the elimination of private enterprise in 1929. The 'means of production' were definitively 'socialized' in Stalin's Great Turn that began in that year, but how and when 'socialism' would turn into 'communism' was not specified in the 1936 constitution. A somewhat half-cocked effort to answers these questions was made in the new (third) Communist Party

Programme adopted in 1961, which announced the building of communism in the Soviet Union within twenty years. This was a rather radical departure from Marx's theories, for it went unexplained how this could happen in a world of countries of which a mere one-third were ruled by communist parties. More concretely, confusion about the expansion of communism soon after 1917 is palpable from the anaemic existence of international organizations that were to further the cause: after the dissolution of the Communist International (*Comintern*) in 1943 – it lasted not even a quarter of a century – and the tacit disappearance of the Communist Information Bureau (*Cominform*) in 1949, a mere two years after it had been created, the Warsaw Pact was founded in 1955, but its task was limited to militarily defending the Soviet Union and Eastern European 'People's Republics' from any Western threat (thus reinforcing Toynbee's argument about the priority of defence). It was by no means an organization on the basis of which a larger communist empire could be created, or, indeed, an instrument intended to expand communist rule elsewhere. And the coup in 1917, as well as the early survival of Soviet Russia, was almost entirely the result of supreme opportunism and sheer luck, not of any grand strategy.[7] In addition, the Bolshevik takeover of Russia was not intended as an attempt to restore the Russian empire, but as a stepping stone towards the global triumph of communism.[8]

Ultimately, then, the Russian and Soviet empires, too, were accidents of history, rather than the consequence of a deliberate long-term strategy. Indeed, most empires are to some extent. Only Hitler and Mussolini seem to have mapped out very deliberate plans to carve out an empire (indeed, divide up the world), but their cases seem to prove that most viable empires are products of long-term historical developments, some of which are willed, while others are accidental. Certainly, the Russian and Soviet empires have been among the largest the world has ever seen, but like that of the Chingisids, the Spaniards, or Alexander, this was mainly because Russian conquerors battled militarily weak opponents, or moved into regions that were sparsely inhabited and could easily be claimed, not because of their rulers' megalomania.

3

The Russian Empire in Western Eyes

Human beings are fundamentally alike, even if the vagaries of history and culture make others sometimes seem exceedingly different. In its investigation of the past to explain the present, the study of history is so valuable because it can help us understand the current behaviour of ourselves and our societies – or others and their communities – that at first sight might seem odd or incomprehensible. Rather than dismissing others as fundamentally and irreparably flawed, such a historically infused sensitivity about others can inform useful attempts to create a better world. Unfortunately, Western discourse about Russia has frequently lacked such sensitivity: too often, Westerners reduced Russia's culture to a caricature, and its people to a bunch of aliens hailing from a different galaxy rather than fellow human beings. The image of the Russian state as a sort of everlasting empire with incessant expansionist ambitions, and as an eternal threat to Europe or the West, has often been due more to the eye of the beholder than based on actual observable facts. The words of the Russian writer Vladimir Maksimov (1930–1995), an Orthodox Christian conservative who was chased out of the Soviet Union, come to mind.[1] After the 1991 Soviet crash, Maksimov returned to the Russian Federation, and dejectedly announced on television that 'Russia has no friends,' nor had it ever had any. The message was that at the slightest trespass made by any Russian, everyone immediately demonized all of the Russians for this unpardonable misdeed.

Toynbee would agree. In his understanding of history, Russia was the perfect foil for the West, the anti-West or the other civilization. To what the Anglo-American world believed in the early days of the Cold War, Toynbee countered that Russia was neither aggressor nor imperialist power: as it always had been forced to do, it was defending itself from foreign predators. Oddly, Toynbee echoed Stalin's words, uttered when in 1931 the Soviet dictator offered a rationale behind the ruthless implementation of the First Five Year Plan.[2] Even so, Toynbee was not wrong about Russia being harassed by aggressive foes, and frequently being seen only in the blackest of terms by those casting about for a foil.

And little has changed in this regard, perhaps.[3] Without making it all right, the recent behaviour of the Putin government with regards to Crimea and eastern Ukraine does at least become more intelligible if seen in the light of Russian alarm about the expansion of the North Atlantic Treaty Organization (NATO) to the very border of the Russian Federation, after the Baltic states joined this military alliance in 2004. This was followed by Ukraine casting covetous eyes towards the EU, as did Georgia: it was no longer too outlandish to ponder the possibility of their EU or even NATO membership, as Estonia, Lithuania and Latvia had received. A glance at the map shows that European Russia would then be caught in a NATO pincer that would absorb Moscow and St Petersburg if it closed.

Despite Toynbee's perceptive criticism regarding the concept of innate or immutable Russian aggression, then, an echo of this essentialized image of a consciously planned empire that strives for European or even global hegemony is still a common trope even in Western scholarship about today's Russia, long after the fall of the Soviet Union (and, clearly, to some extent the conventional wisdom infusing Western discourse, not just of politicians and journalists, but also of those who prefer to rely on social media for their political fix). At the beginning of this millennium, the historian John LeDonne suggested that, from the seventeenth century onward, the expansion of the Romanov Empire was driven by something akin to a long-term grand strategy, aiming to find defensible borders.[4] This was the source of the aggression that eventually led Russians to the shores of the Pacific Ocean and the Caspian, Black, Baltic and White Seas, as well as to the Altai Heights and the Caucasus.

Discussions about grand strategies along the lines of contemporary designs proposed by the French King Henri IV's advisor, the Duc de Sully (1560–1641), Oliver Cromwell's Western Design of the 1650s, or the Dutch *Groot Dessein* of the 1620s to dominate the Americas, were indeed *en vogue* in the seventeenth century, and may have occurred in the Kremlin of the Tsars Mikhail (r. 1613–45) and Aleksei (r. 1645–76). The porous Muscovite borders with the steppe borderlands had been an on-going concern that had led to the construction of a fortified line south of Moscow, while invasions from the west in the early seventeenth-century Troubles made the early Romanovs acutely aware of their country's vulnerability to foreign encroachment. But while the seventeenth-century Western powers' drafting of plans hardly meant acting upon them, the early Romanovs could barely conceive of a Russia demarcated by natural borders, let alone contemplate the execution of any grand strategy.

Indeed, at the Treaty of Tordesillas in 1494 Spain and Portugal had agreed on a brazen strategy to divide up the world – informed by a good deal of ignorance about its size – between each other. Once it occupied Portugal in 1580, Spain could theoretically lay claim to all of the globe outside Europe. Within Europe there was no question of Spain's political hegemony, however. For, besides the pope, who was the spiritual leader of all of Western Christendom (at least before 1517), the secular overlord of this community of believers was the Holy Roman emperor, who in 1580 was not the same person as the king of Spain, even if the two monarchs happened to be relatives. Only 25 years earlier, Charles v (1500–1558) had been both Holy Roman emperor and Spanish king (and carried a whole bunch of further titles), and had ruled the Spanish maritime possessions. His was in theory the largest European-led empire that existed in history before the British or Russian empires of the nineteenth century, but his power was in many of his territories exactly that, more theoretical than real.[5] Charles concluded at the end of his life that it was better to abandon any pretence at universal hegemony, believing that by giving his son and his brother each about half of his empire they might have a better chance of enforcing their rule than he had enjoyed.

There is no doubt that the desire to unify the world under their thumb has repeatedly been expressed by the rulers of the larger empires that have arisen in human history, but to accomplish this ambition has ever proved impossible. China's ruling dynasties solved this problem by pretending that their country formed the centre of the world to which all others were subordinate (once in a while demanding tribute), while the Romans suggested that everyone outside the *limes* was a savage or barbarian animal not worthy of being ruled by the eternal city.

The West (especially the British, French and Americans) has since the nineteenth century tried to impose a sort of uniform political and economic system on the rest of the world and almost seemed to have achieved global hegemony at the end of the Cold War. Today, however, it appears fairly obvious that the triumph of the Western way in the world is still far off.

Hitler's New Order was another stab at world domination that fell far short and was brief despite its brutality. And for more than a millennium both Christians and Muslims have tried to conquer the world in the name of their religion, but neither has become the religion of the majority of the world's population. Many, then, tried to acquire global supremacy, but no one came anywhere close. And while many strove at least in theory for supremacy over large parts of the world, very few developed concrete or realistic plans to accomplish such absolute hegemony. In the Russian case, only the Soviet period witnessed such an attempt, although it remained mainly theoretical, as we saw. Largely, empires come about through happenstance, emerging almost accidentally. Whenever a Napoléon or Hitler tried to follow a blueprint in creating an empire, they soon met insurmountable obstacles that forced them to give up their plans, and swiftly cost them their power altogether. Chingis Khan and his descendants, who played a crucial role in Russian history, did not exactly set forth to carve out an empire from the Pacific to the Mediterranean. Like Alexander the Great, they had the good fortune that throughout Eurasia no one was able to stop their mounted assault.

Around 1520, Charles v appeared to have a chance to unite Western Christendom under his rule like a latter-day Charlemagne, but only because he inherited most of his realm rather than winning it by use of military force could he even consider such a strategy. Once he tried to expand further the yield was meagre. He acknowledged the futility of most of his strivings at the end of his life and retired to a monastery. He had made little to no headway against the Ottoman Turks, the French, or Luther, and deemed it wise to divide up the lands that he actually had ruled between his brother and his son.

Charles's conundrum brings us back to Russia's early modern age, the era of the last Riurikids (Ivan III, Vasily III and Ivan IV) and the first Romanovs (Mikhail and Aleksei). Their politics were moulded by similar contemporaneous eschatological ideas of a universal empire of sorts, Orthodox rather than Catholic (as in Charles's case). But in the sixteenth century, Russia's fate still hung in the balance: in an odd coincidence, in the very same year of 1583 the Russian outlet on the Baltic Sea at Narva was given up while the first Russian bridgehead in Siberia was established. And then the Time of Troubles engulfed the tsar's empire. Once order was restored, in early Romanov Moscow the execution of any grand strategy towards empire was likely considered as far-fetched as the French, English or Dutch found it to be in the seventeenth century. In the context of their state's already considerable size, and of a past when Eastern Slavonic princes ruled areas that neither Mikhail nor Aleksei ruled before 1650, ideas of (re-)gathering the lands of historical Rus' indubitably existed at those tsars' court. Kyiv, however, was seemingly firmly located within the domains of the Polish-Lithuanian Commonwealth. And once Aleksei decided that he could make a play for Kyiv after 1650, his motivation was before all that of religion, as Orthodoxy in Ukraine was threatened by Catholicism. Any dreams of even regional domination were quashed, especially by Swedish power.

Because it had an important religious component, one might suggest that Russian expansionism was of a different character to that of the more secular seventeenth-century English, French or Dutch designs. In response to the writings by Nikolai Berdyaev of the first half of the twentieth century, scholars have weighed the importance of the concept of Russians identifying themselves as the acolytes of Moscow in its guise as the third and last 'Rome' before the Apocalypse. This ideology was developed by a Pskov monk named Filofei (1465–1542) somewhere in the early 1500s. Berdyaev's suggestion that his ideas exerted great influence over the tsar's actions has by now been rejected by most historians, however.

Still, that the Russians of the Moscow region had a kind of siege mentality after the fall of Constantinople in 1453 cannot be denied. While the Muscovites were freeing themselves from more than two hundred years of Mongolian-Tatar (Muslim) rule, all of the rest of Eastern Orthodox Christianity had fallen subject to a Muslim (Turkish-Ottoman) ruler. Thus the impetus behind the expansionism of the early modern tsars was rather more religious than military-political or military-geographical. Its aim was to carve out and defend a new independent centre of Orthodoxy. The early campaigns by Ivan IV, who conquered the Muslim khanates along the Volga during the 1550s, seem to confirm this religious inspiration (even if they, too, hint at the later Riurikids' desire to claim the Mongolian succession).

The jury is still out on whether or not Ivan IV thought of himself either as a Christian version of a Tatar khan or a latter-day Byzantine emperor who championed true Christianity in preparation for the Last Judgement. Indeed, he may have veered between both ideas, and he may have also been no more than a pragmatic 'new monarch' in the European style, such as Louis XI (r. 1461–83) of France or Henry VII (r. 1485–1509) of England, trying to create a viable state with defensible borders and acquiring or establishing ports at the White, Baltic and Caspian Seas that could stimulate trade. He certainly seems to have refrained from stirring up any religious conflict with his numerous new Muslim subjects, which would have been unwise given limited Russian strength. Somewhat luckily, Ivan avoided a major battle with the Ottoman sultan's forces and their Crimean-Tatar allies who, during the 1560s, tried to come to the rescue of their Muslim co-religionists in Astrakhan and Kazan. The Tatars sacked Moscow in 1571, and even though they did not stay and the Russians recovered afterwards, any anti-Islamic policies must have seemed foolish even to this notoriously labile tsar.

To perceive a truly coherent long-term religiously driven strategy behind Ivan IV's or the early Romanovs' carving out of a Russian (Orthodox) empire is belied by their actions, which are much more impulsive than betraying any clear plan, reactive more than autonomously driven. Ivan IV turned from fighting Tatars along the Volga to fighting Livonian knights in the Baltic region, attempting to conquer territory that was claimed by other Christians (albeit not Orthodox). He ignored the fate of the many Orthodox Christians ruled by the Polish king (who doubled as Lithuanian grand duke). Mikhail Romanov and his son Aleksei did try to (re-)conquer Polish-Lithuanian-held territory in which the population was predominantly Orthodox, but the Smolensk War of 1632–4 and the Thirteen Years War of 1654–67 had far more immediate causes: to recover the Polish gains of the early part of the century, as confirmed by the 1618 Truce of Deulino, and to counter the Union of Brest of 1596, which tempted Orthodox believers to submit to the Catholic pope. This caused great unrest among Orthodox clergy and lay people in Ukraine and Belarus. The otherwise cautious Aleksei was persuaded by Ukrainian pleas (not least by some of the Ukrainian Orthodox clerics) to throw the dice and attack Poland in 1654, although the memory of his father's failure at recovering Smolensk played a role as well.

As with Ivan IV, pragmatism seemed to have been Aleksei's leitmotiv. It is a truism to suggest that monarchs before the modern age were judged by their military prowess and rated themselves using criteria of military success. Certainly, Ivan IV (and Ivan III before him) or Aleksei, as soon as they took the reins, bristled with the desire to fight a war, and so they did, covering themselves in glory, at least initially. Mikhail Romanov is the exception here, but even he was persuaded to seek retribution from the Poles, at a time when this should have seemed foolhardy.

After his coronation in 1613, Mikhail had first been forced to concede painful territorial losses at Stolbovo to the Swedes in 1617 and at Deulino the next year to the Poles. Only very cautiously did he test Polish resolve in 1632, and his quick withdrawal from the Smolensk War after a severe military defeat is a sign of his smarts.[6] When Mikhail was offered by Orthodox Cossacks the sovereignty over Azov in 1642, he carefully consulted with his *boyar*s and rejected the offer, afraid to end up in an all-out war with Crimean Tatars and Ottoman Turks.[7] But Mikhail may have played a risky game: after his death in 1645, a cascade of unrest overtook Russia, threatening the very survival of the dynasty between 1645 and 1650. It may be that Mikhail's excessive caution undermined the authority of the tsar among his subjects. For a few years, the eruption of a new Time of Troubles seemed possible.

Aleksei went to war, though, and met with a good deal of success; subsequently, he made considerable headway in bringing Ukrainian Orthodox believers under the rule of Moscow through the 1667 Andrusovo Treaty. But he could not dislodge the Swedes from control over the Baltic littoral, through which Russia's main seaport with Western Europe remained frosty Arkhangel'sk until the early 1700s. Can we perceive any grand strategy in the military campaigns or wars of these three early modern tsars? Is there some sort of constant that can be detected in their foreign policy or warfare that betrays a coherent drive towards empire? Again, calculated pragmatism rather than grandiose planning underscored their moves.

Certainly, much of Russian foreign policy in the direction of their southern borderlands (*Okraina* was the Slavonic term used for them) was defensive, directed before the middle of the eighteenth century against raids by the Crimean Tatars, who were the sultan's allies. There was little that was 'imperialist' about these Muscovite policies, as exemplified in the building of the hundreds-of-kilometres-long southern fortified frontier in the sixteenth and seventeenth centuries.[8] Perhaps the best counter-evidence to any concerted efforts guided by the tsar and his advisors is the happenstance manner in which Siberia was claimed between 1583 and 1642.

Certainly until the final years of Catherine the Great's rule the location of most of Russia's borders in Europe remained opaque (its western border with east-central Europe has never been very obvious), and this was even longer the case in Inner Asia. Indeed, beyond the Caspian Sea, it is very difficult to identify any 'natural borders' (in itself a concept only born in the French Enlightenment) that could separate Turkestan (Central Asia) from Iran, Afghanistan or western China.

In the 1690s, after personally taking the reins in Muscovy, Peter the Great briefly flirted with the Holy League, an alliance of Catholic monarchs under the pope's auspices that tried to end the Ottoman Empire in Europe. He joined this effort too late, however, to make much of a difference. In Peter's correspondence one encounters bold statements about leading a crusade against the Turkish sultan, but Peter spent much more energy fighting fellow Christian monarchs and was painfully rebuffed by the Turks at the Battle of the Pruth in 1711. Peter, of course, did reconceive Russia as an empire in the Western style, but in a peculiar manner: he seemed rather more keen on building a maritime empire than a land-based one. If this was a grand strategy, it was a new one, having little to do with a search for defensible natural borders. His long war with Sweden of 1700 to 1721 was primarily aimed at controlling a good slice of the Baltic coast to accommodate a navy and merchant marine. Again, though, as with his ancestors, pragmatism (and avoiding loss of face) and opportunism informed Peter's moves, too. Thus the somewhat incongruous Persian campaign of 1722–3: Iran had descended into chaos, and suddenly a fine opportunity to control much of the Caspian littoral offered itself.

Peter was still mainly interested in being offered a place at Europe's table as the monarch of a Great Power rather than as an emperor. He received the title of *imperator* in 1721 from a sycophantic Russian Senate, but seems to have been less than confident that he was a true emperor. There were some other plays for a type of Western imperial status, as expressed in the quasi-Roman triumphal parade after the capture of Azov in

1696, but the Roman tradition sat ill with a culture of which the tradition was much more Greek or neo-Hellenistic. The humiliation of the Battle of the Pruth and the dressing down by the Chinese through the 1689 Treaty of Nerchinsk were moments that reminded Peter that Russia did not quite match the greatest empires of history.

Catherine II's reign witnessed an unresolved contradiction between a ruler who was an all-European Enlightenment figure of sorts who championed education and sought substantive legal reform, while reigning as an autocrat who somewhat accidentally became one of the most successful military conquerors in Russian history. Finally gaining the upper hand over Tatars and Turks and destroying Poland-Lithuania, she added territory after territory, but proved a tolerant ruler in terms of religion. She resolutely rejected any efforts to proselytize Orthodoxy among her new subjects, allowing them to keep their faith, even the Jews of 'New Russia' and its surrounding areas. A grand strategy behind the creation of Russia's empire does not match the specifics of her reign, for Catherine's territorial acquisitions were driven by opportunism, facing an Ottoman Empire that began to show weakness and a Rzeczpospolita (the Polish state) that was falling apart.

Like Peter, Catherine came up with a grand design of a sort of her own: like Peter's plans, however, hers was an almost wholly new idea that was to guide the direction of Russia's foreign policy, not an effort to pick up where her predecessors had left off. This so-called Greek project aimed at making the Black Sea into some sort of Russian lake and Istanbul the capital of a companion Christian empire to Russia's, ruled by her second grandson, who was fittingly baptized Constantine.

Catherine's armies were far more successful against the Ottoman military than those of her predecessors, but any further advances towards Istanbul after the landmark peace of Kuchuk Kainarji (1774) were thwarted. Austria proved a reluctant ally in the effort to execute Catherine's designs, and more urgent issues such as developments in France and Poland distracted Catherine, while age began to take its toll on the empress.

The seventeenth- and eighteenth-century Romanovs were not out to establish their hegemony over Europe and Asia, or to conquer contingent territory from coast to coast or mountain to coast. They did try to create an empire that could defend itself against all its foes through its own military and economic means. This search for a self-sufficient empire is, in fact, much more of a constant in Russian and Soviet history from Ivan III until today than a strategy to dominate the world.

Modern Russia's imperial rise was not planned. A discrete sequence of events led to its expansion into the largest empire in the world. Frequently, this growth occurred because of its neighbours crumbling, when the tsars replaced other potentates who could no longer guarantee order and stability to the local population, a strange echo of the first legendary invitation of the Slavs to the Varangians as relayed in Kyiv's *Primary Chronicle* (*Povest' vremennykh let*). This happened across Siberia, in the Baltic region, in Ukraine and the Caucasus, and even in Peter's campaign in Iran. And so had the Vikings, Mongols, Teutonic Knights or Lithuanians acted before them when they descried a region in which disorder was rampant and imposed their rule over the eastern Slavs, Baltic peoples, or Finno-Ugrians of the Eastern European Plain.

Ultimately, the Western reading of Russia as an, or the, evil empire is a rhetorical trope, a myth, often based on lazy or simplistic thinking and frequently a foil useful for domestic consumption. From different angles, and looking at different periods, Marshall Poe and Larry Wolff have tried to pinpoint the genesis of Russia or Russians as antipodes to Europe or the West in Western and Central European writing.[9] Poe proposed that Western travellers such as Sigismund von Herberstein (1486–1566), Giles Fletcher (*c.* 1548–1611) and Adam Olearius (1599–1671) wrote authoritative texts that determined the Western view of Russia in the sixteenth and seventeenth centuries. Interestingly, Poe suggests that while these texts contain a pat series of clichés about other cultures, these travellers, because they had seen the country themselves, did not entirely misrepresent Muscovy under Vasily III, Ivan IV, Fyodor I or Mikhail. Prejudiced they undoubtedly were, but they found their preconceived notions confirmed once they crossed the border into the tsar's realm.

But did they truly throw off their cultural blinkers? Did they not merely see what their own reading had taught them to see? Olearius or Fletcher did not speak Russian, and Herberstein only haltingly so, and visitors were hardly ever given permission to freely intermingle with the Russians before 1700. Despite this linguistic handicap, their accounts became authoritative. Wolff suggests that the Western idea of Eastern Europe (in which Russia loomed ever larger) became enshrined in the eighteenth-century Enlightenment as a sort of anti-Western Europe. Again, even if some of the contours of the Enlightenment's Eastern Europe consisted more of rhetoric than reality, Wolff does point out that, if one moved eastward on the European continent after 1700, one gradually moved into a sparsely populated, rural region in which most labour was unfree and aristocracy and monarchs ruled unchallenged, a contrast to what prevailed in densely populated Western Europe. The question might be asked whether or not Poe's travellers observed a different Russia from Wolff's. They probably should have: many scholars of Russia (Russian or not) tend to agree one way or another that the effective reign of Peter the Great (1689–1725) provided a watershed, the outcome being a wholly different Petrine or post-Petrine empire. But was the caricature of Russia by then so ingrained that descriptions of it fell back on pre-Petrine treatises that had been popular in the West? Poe argues that Westerners thought of Russians as 'a people born to slavery' before 1700, while Lloyd Berry and Robert Crummey named one of their books 'rude and barbarous kingdom', referring to another dismissive description of Muscovy during that era.[10]

The hostile image of nineteenth-century Russia (which was diffused only after Waterloo) seems a legacy of the anti-West that Poe and Wolff depict of early modern Russia, and Ronald Reagan's condemnation of the Soviet Union as the 'evil empire' seamlessly fits the pattern as a further iteration of this caricature. Indeed, especially since 2014 many an armchair foreign-policy expert appears to have jumped almost with relief at the opportunity offered by the ill-conceived Crimean annexation and the Russian interference in eastern Ukraine to depict Russia once more as the eternal aggressive empire.

4
Prehistory and Geography: Rus'

Geography is not destiny, despite facile ideas about the influence of climate on politics or culture that have been in vogue since at least Montesquieu (1689–1755), who in fact suggested that Russians were insensitive because of the cold climate in which they lived.[1] But geography does influence history. Safety and security to engage in settled agriculture seems to have been behind the initial desire of the Eastern Slav communities that began to settle across the Eastern European Plain somewhere in the eighth and ninth centuries of our era, far away from a temperate climate that is much more conducive to crop cultivation. They had earlier belonged to a territorially linked Slavonic population inhabiting the region of today's northwest Ukraine and southwest Belarus (more or less in and around the Pripet marshes) that became separated through various out-migrations and the settlement of others between them.[2] Perhaps the swampland offered protection from the Huns, Avars or Magyars and other aggressive nomads, who began to roam across the grasslands (*steppe*) north of the Black Sea in an era when the global climate cooled down significantly, after approximately 400 CE.[3] Despite their treacherous nature, the Pripet morasses have been traversed by large Polish, German, French and Russian armies, so true safety may not have been achieved; the territory north of these marshlands might have seemed more promising in this regard. This was land quite remote, with a severely inhospitable climate, avoided by most trekking from Asia in the direction of Europe. Perhaps the Slavs migrated in search of drier soil more suited to plant crops than the water-logged region of the marshes, or they did so since they practised slash-and-burn techniques, which drain the soil of its nutrients, forcing them to migrate every several years. It appears, too, that various Slavonic communities occupied lands to the south of the Pripet swamps that had been vacated by those who had fled from, or been butchered by, migrating nomadic warriors.[4] They consequently morphed into three main groups: Eastern, Western and Southern Slavs. Their separation from each other became more defined once other peoples settled between them, while each of the three subgroups mixed with differing neighbouring peoples as well.

In the absence of any serious elevation (even the Urals can be relatively easily scaled, its highest mountain not even reaching 1,900 metres) the East European Plain and northwestern Asia were relatively easy to traverse on horseback, and the terrain was equally well suited to those using boats and rafts. It was criss-crossed by rivers, frequently running close together, linked by portages, overland carry routes short enough to make it possible to haul small vessels and goods to the next waterway and continue one's travels. Scandinavians seem to have been the first to develop consummate skill in this manner of moving around using the waterways; they appeared not only in Western Europe but in Eastern Europe in the age of the Vikings that began in the ninth century. It may be that gradually warming weather made the rivers navigable for longer periods than previously, so that this manner of travelling became more feasible.

In a somewhat bizarre legend first recorded a quarter of a millennium after the events had allegedly taken place, Eastern Slavs asked 'Varangians' (who have been identified as Swedish Vikings) to establish order among them in the middle of the ninth century. As with the story about peaceful Finnish-Slav miscegenation in central and northern Russia some centuries later that Kliuchevskii suggested, one suspects that the arrival of the Vikings was less enthusiastically welcomed on the part of the Slavs than recorded by the monks who reported it in the *Primary Chronicle*, some 250 years later in the early twelfth century.[5] Viking violence harassed the local population, whether in coastal northwestern Europe or along the banks of east European rivers. The Vikings, as they did in Britain, Ireland or France, eventually retired from raiding and settled from Novgorod near the Baltic Sea in the north to Kyiv on the Dnipro river in the south. Viking plunderers became lords over their Slavic subjects. Within a few generations, they adopted the local language and culture, rather than imposing theirs on those they had vanquished. This acculturation is not unlike what occurred in Normandy, or the Danelaw.

The Vikings' arrival is recorded in contemporary Byzantine sources that tell of people having come from Rus' – by which they meant the area of what is now more or less western Russia, Belarus and northern Ukraine – to Constantinople around 900. Several trade treaties were concluded, which the Varangians mainly signed with unmistakably Scandinavian names; they traded in honey, wax and furs, but also in slaves, whom they picked out from among the Slavs over whom they ruled.

A measure of stability seems to have been established within Varangian Rus' in the later ninth and early tenth centuries. Enough unity of purpose among the Rus' principalities was found to ally in defence of Eastern Slav territory against a wide array of foes, including the ethnically Turkic and religiously Judaic Khazars who had settled in the region of the Don delta at the Black Sea and the Volga estuary at the Caspian Sea.[6] Other foes were Turkic nomads hailing from Middle Asia, latter-day successors to Huns, Avars and Magyars. The Byzantine emperor lent some support to these efforts after the foremost Rus' chief, Volodymyr (Vladimir) of Kyiv (*c.* 960–1015), converted to Orthodox Christianity in 988. From that point onward, Greek clergy began to proselytize more intensively among the pagan Slavs, and the Greek church and Byzantine political culture provided the tools to forge a somewhat better organized and coherent polity, uniting the various Rus' communities.

But this predominantly Eastern Slav state, known to historians as Kyivan Rus' (after its capital Kyiv), was brittle, not least because primitive means of transport and communication made it hard to rule a state that acquired a significant size around the year 1000. The town of Novgorod and its hinterland, 800 to 900 kilometres away from Volodymyr's capital, seems to have existed almost independently from Kyiv. The Vladimir-Suzdal' region, in which Moscow was founded, was as far away from Kyiv, and often could defy its grand duke or grand prince (*velikii kniaz*) with impunity.

Besides being undermined by these enormous distances, cohesion was jeopardized by the custom of partible inheritance as followed by the Eastern Slavic princes. Especially after the early twelfth century, their realm tended to remain divided up into several smaller duchies, none of which obeyed the grand duke for any great length of time.[7] Efforts (not least by the Orthodox Church, whose key motive for writing the *Primary*

Chronicle was to benefit Rus' unity, for example) to maintain a unified country failed. Kyivan Rus' was a state in which the grand prince enjoyed suzerainty (nominal power) rather than sovereignty (true authority) over the various principalities that officially deferred to him, as the successor of the mythical Riurik. Riurik was the Viking who according to legend was the first to firmly rule them all in the ninth century. His descendants all carried the title of prince or *kniaz* for centuries after.

Kyivan Rus', which stretched from the Black Sea to Lake Ladoga, and from the Dniestr river to the confluence of the Oka and Volga rivers, a distance of some 1,500 kilometres from its northern to its southernmost reaches, and some 800 kilometres from its eastern to its western borderlands, was on paper the largest state in Europe. But while it shares this distinction with early modern or modern Russia, only a few other traits of those Russias may be recognizable in Rus': the use of a form of an Eastern-Slavonic tongue (proto-Ukrainian-Russian-Belarusian) as its administrative and church language; an (albeit often weak) attachment to Christianity of the Eastern Orthodox tradition after 988; and its location on roughly the same territory as the later Russian, Belarusian and Ukrainian heartlands. To consider Kyivan Rus' as the ancestor of the tsars' or Putin's empire is an ahistorical and nationalist misreading of history *wie es eigentlich gewesen ist*,[8] and as dubious as seeing late Imperial Rome (let's say after the emperor Diocletian's rule) as the ancestor of the modern British Empire because of its religion, its settlement of colonies abroad and its capital's location in Europe. Rus' was not in any profound sense a coherent state: far more than any other polity that bore the name of 'empire', it resembles at most the post-1648 Holy Roman Empire, an empire only in name.

Nonetheless, ruling circles and ideologists in Muscovy, ever broadening layers of the population in Imperial Russia and the Soviet Union, and, finally, many citizens of post-Soviet Russia, saw or see Rus' as the original Russian empire. Ironically, in Ukraine, too, many see Rus' as the first incarnation of their nation-state.

5

The Mongols, Siberia and Asia

In Rus', quarrels about inheritance were common among the Riurikid princes and led to internecine warfare, while various enemies from the outside further contributed to a restless existence for all who lived on a territory that included most of today's Ukraine, Belarus, and central and northwestern European Russia. Despite frequent violent conflict, trade both at home and abroad was conducted in a fairly high volume compared with other parts of contemporary medieval Europe, facilitated by the convenient network of waterways of reasonably navigable rivers (and the few fairly friendly portages that connected the western Dvina with the Dnipro/Dniepr and the Volga) that drained into the Baltic, Black and Caspian Seas. Thus, even if the mainstay of the Slavic population's livelihood was sedentary agriculture, the number of towns in Rus' was not inconsiderable, and enough surplus wealth was generated to allow for the creation of some impressive cultural hallmarks, such as the elaborately decorated Caves Monastery (Pecherskaya Lavra) at Kyiv. In addition, laws were codified and some chronicles written which, besides marking the observation of important religious holidays, recorded some of the mythical and factual history of the Eastern Slavs. And some Rus' princesses married into other ruling houses in Europe as well.

But throughout the existence of Kyivan Rus' as an organized state or conglomerate of states, which may be said to have been from about 950 to 1242, a stark problem presented itself for which no solution was found until the building of the fortified border in southern Muscovy in the sixteenth and seventeenth centuries: its borders were porous, open really, and its lands were easily and frequently overrun by invaders. As noted, the Ural mountains are not particularly high and can be fairly easily crossed, but, even more significantly, a large gap between their southern foothills and the Caspian Sea exists where no marked natural obstacle – the Iaik (Ural) river was not difficult to cross when frozen in winter – stopped people from moving from the steppe lands of northwestern Asia into those of Eastern Europe.

As William MacNeill suggested, only in the early modern age did sedentary cultures in Eurasia fortify themselves adequately enough to avoid being periodically overwhelmed by marauding nomadic tribes.[1] In Eastern Europe, it took millennia to find an effective way to stave off the mounted warriors. In what seems an endless sequence, Hittites, Scythians, Huns, Avars, Magyars, Polovtsy, Pechenegs, Mongols and Uzbeks criss-crossed the steppe without meeting effective resistance. Before 1700, the Eastern Slavs lived for almost a millennium in the borderlands that bore the first brunt of any nomadic attack launched from Middle Asia into Eastern Europe. Kyivan Rus' was able to deal with Pechenegs and Polovtsy (also known as Kumans), but in the late 1230s proved incapable of dealing with the Mongolian cavalry's rapid invasion. While most of Europe further west was saved by an equally swift withdrawal by the Mongols in 1242 when they returned to their homeland after news of the death of Great Khan Ögödei (1185–1241), the Mongols and their Turkic allies, who became eventually known as Tatars, lorded it over central Russia and the lands along the banks of the Volga for a quarter millennium.[2]

The Tatars lasted for a much shorter period of time – decades rather than centuries – as supreme rulers in lands to the west and south of what is now central Russia, which led to a decisive fork in the road of Eastern Slavic historical development. Those who lived in today's western Ukraine were drawn into the orbit of Poland, while those in Belarus and eastern Ukraine fell under Lithuanian hegemony: as a result, two distinctive languages emerged by about 1500, Russian and Ruthenian, with the latter gradually further splitting into two vernacular tongues, Belarusian and Ukrainian. Different forms of written language (sometimes called Chancery Slavonic) also evolved, rooted in the religious language that is known as Old Church Slavonic, which was developed before 1000 by Orthodox churchmen to facilitate the conversion of the Slavs.

After 1240, the previous regular exposure to the violence of Asian invaders was followed for eight generations of Russians by relatively tranquil Mongolian rule (even if internecine warfare among the Chingisids occasionally flared up). But the Tatars adopted Islam as their creed, a religion to which Orthodox Christians had been hostile for centuries. More than anything, it was the Orthodox Church that between the 1240s and 1480 kept a desire to regain independence alive among the Russians.

The waves of Asian invaders that culminated in Mongolian rule informed the deeply felt Russian yearning for better defensible borders, long after the Tatars had been ousted from the Russian heartland (although Crimean Tatars raided Russian lands into the eighteenth century). But finding such borders in an eastward direction proved impossible: until the very shores of the Pacific Ocean, most of the terrain beyond the Urals is

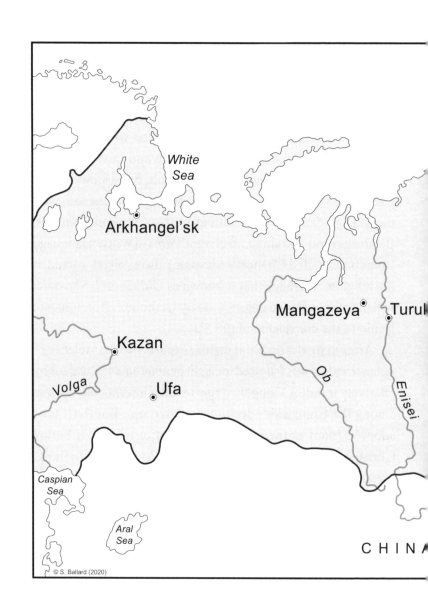

Russia's 17th-century expansion into northern Asia.

flat, and the Ob, Lena and Enisei rivers and their tributaries could be traversed when frozen in winter. Although fur hunting may have been more important than anything in causing the conquest of Siberia before 1700, the desire for safe borders was never quite lost in the expansionist drive hallmarking Russian history for most of the second half of the second millennium.

As part of a sort of sustained counter-attack on the various khanates into which the Tatar Golden Horde dissolved after 1500, the khanate of Sibir on the eastern side of the Ural mountains was conquered by the 1590s. In addition, the Muscovites gradually erected a defensive fortification line all the way from the Lithuanian border to the Volga and across to the Urals in the sixteenth and seventeenth centuries to hinder the endemic raids by Crimean Tatars (who until 1783 tenaciously survived as a latter-day western outpost of the Chingisid empire) onto Muscovite territory. This Russian version of the Great Wall of China combined natural obstacles, such as dense forest or waterways, with checkpoints and fortresses. How effective it was remains a matter of debate. Tatar raids from the south declined in the second half of the seventeenth century, but it seems that was, more than anything else, because Moscow began to control a significant part of Ukraine. It may very well be that increasing Cossack strength during the seventeenth century was another cause of the decline of Crimean Tatar raids on Muscovite territory. The fortified line appears to have done little to hinder the various rebels that advanced on Moscow during the early seventeenth-century Time of Troubles, or to stop the Cossacks of Stepan Razin crossing into Russian territory in 1670.

The rapid conquest of Siberia after 1580 (the Pacific was reached around 1640) was due in part to eastward travel being facilitated by using waterways, copying the Viking advance into Eastern Europe during the 800s. Proclaiming Russian sovereignty was made easy by the spread of diseases that decimated an already small indigenous Siberian population. The Muscovites, many of whom were Cossacks – that is, freebooting warriors who descended from runaway serfs and were hired as mercenaries by the tsarist government – behaved with brutality if they met resistance. The Siberians often lived in isolated communities, and had usually no answer to the firepower of the Russian conquerors.

Rather than a search for some sort of natural border for Muscovy, Siberia's conquest was largely caused by an insatiable appetite for animal hides. Siberian fur was in high demand in the seventeenth century, not just in Russia itself but in Central and Western Europe as well. Dutch, English and other traders keenly purchased from the Russians the ermine, sable, marten and other precious furs that were in even greater demand than the popular North American beaver hides in seventeenth-century Europe. While the Russians in Siberia did trap and hunt fur-bearing animals themselves, they adopted the hostage system from their Tatar predecessors to increase their pelt harvests. Indigenous communities had to surrender some of their own people to the occupants of the Russian fortresses strewn across Siberia. These hostages were released once the annual fur tribute (*yasak*) was delivered, only to have the process recommence a few months later.

Here another parallel with a different period of Russian imperialist history may be found, that of Russia's expansion into middle Asia in the nineteenth century. For with regards to that territorial expansion, too, the initiative was taken by almost independently operating Russian military officers who staked a claim over land and people previously ruled by Muslim chiefs. With their obsolete military forces, those traditional rulers had little to no chance in fighting well-armed and trained Russian troops.

But this was much later. In the seventeenth century, the Kazak Hordes that controlled the regions east of the Caspian Sea, and the Uzbek or Turkmen population beyond them, were still too strong an opponent for any expansion to occur south of Siberia proper. After the Siberian fur-bearing animals had been hunted well-nigh to extinction by 1700, Siberia had little to offer to the Russians before the true beginnings of Russian industrialization in the 1870s. Some mining was undertaken in western Siberia, which reached a considerable scale in the eighteenth century when compared with the contemporaneous mining of iron ore in other countries, but the yields remained minute beside those of the modern era. Siberia became in the seventeenth century a place of exile for Russian political prisoners (one of the first was the Croatian Juraj Krizanich, *c.* 1618–1683), while in the Great Northern War of 1700–1721 prisoners of war were interned beyond the Urals. But most of Siberia remained for the Russians a rather useless frozen tundra and taiga before 1800. In this, too, a parallel with nineteenth-century Central Asia may be observed. When the Russians took over there, any significant trade had declined since the Silk Road(s) had become defunct owing to overseas shipping and railroads. The area developed some cotton cultivation, but Russian textile mills were located too far away to make the industry efficient so expensive railways first needed to be laid down. Middle Asia, too, was a sort of barren wasteland: in its case, more of an arid desert. Russian administrative centres were dotted across both pre-1800 Siberia and pre-1914 Central Asia, with a local

Orthodox hermit in Siberia, 1910.

An ancient cemetery in Central Asia near the Syr-Daria river.

population that went about its business evading the Russian officials and soldiers as much as possible.

The Muscovite explorer Erofei Khabarov (*c.* 1603–*c.* 1671) attempted to expand Russian authority to an area along the Pacific littoral far enough in a southern direction to allow for viable agriculture and the foundation of a port from which ships might sail towards Japan and China. Once the Qing dynasty (1642–1911) became firmly established in Beijing, however, the government, now under the control of ethnic Manchurians whose land of origin was located nearby, checked the Russian advance. In 1689, Russian and Chinese diplomats, both accompanied by a significant military force, concluded the Treaty of Nerchinsk. The two sides agreed to peaceful trade, but the agreement meant that Russia was to have no authority in eastern Siberia below the 55th parallel. North of this line, conditions for human settlement were, to put it mildly, rather poor. It later became the location of the most notorious of Stalin's labour camps.

Instead, on the urging of the hyper-curious Peter the Great, explorers in Russian service moved even further north into Kamchatka. In the 1720s the Dane Vitus Bering (1681–1741) sailed in the straits that still bear his name, and not long after the Russians acquired an outpost in Alaska. In the eighteenth century, they descended along the American coast all the way to the San Francisco Bay area. After Peter's death in 1725, scientific curiosity once again took a back seat to a further search for fur-bearing animals in driving the Russians on in these remote regions. But along the American Pacific shore, too, the supply of hides was not inexhaustible. That from a Russian perspective the cake ultimately was not worth the candle is indicated by the 1867 sale of Alaska to the U.S. government.

In Alaska, the Russian Orthodox Church, meanwhile, proved tenacious, surviving the 1867 sale and converting some of the native Alaskan population to Orthodoxy.

While the conquest of vast expanses of territory such as Middle Asia, Alaska or Siberia yielded few, or, at best, short-lived benefits to the Russian government before the twentieth century, especially after 1917, such acquisitions (and, in the case of Alaska, this has been true for the USA) turned out to be of immense consequence. In the twentieth century, technology made most of the region accessible, beginning with railways such as the Transsiberian track completed in the 1900s, and followed by aeroplanes, radios, and all sorts of industrial machinery for mining and drilling.[3] In both Middle Asia and Siberia, vast deposits of oil, gas and other resources began to be mined. This benefits today not only the Russian Federation but Turkmenistan and Kazakhstan, which have become enormously wealthy as a result. In the case of the Central Asian countries, it remains to be seen whether this is a mere temporary affluence: their wealth is almost entirely the consequence of the winning of fossil fuels and the recent high demand for them on the world market. Siberia, though, has a much broader array of raw materials available, which may help the Russian Federation to maintain a more sustained spell of economic prosperity.

Of course, the Asian conquests did have another consequence most pertinent to our topic. As a result of them, Russia became an empire that was part of the Asian political landscape, and became involved in the history of Asia. This meant that it got involved in the Great Game with Britain in the nineteenth century, and subsequently in conflicts with Japan and China. While Russia's complicated relationship with Iran was more a consequence of the unsettled situation in the Caucasian borderlands that lasted for centuries, even in 1979 the Soviet Union's foray into Afghanistan was linked to the Great Game. Britain's post-1945 withdrawal from South Asia combined with the continued Soviet presence in Central Asia caused the Afghan government to drift into the Soviet orbit. The Afghan invasion, though, proved a fiasco, and hastened the collapse of the Soviet Union. The new Russia that arose from its ashes is located far away from the Afghan borders. But Russia continues to play a role in Asia beyond the Caucasus, through its influence in the Central Asian republics and Mongolia, as well as its somewhat complementary relationship with China, with Russian resources fuelling China's mighty manufacturing sector.

6

Moscow's Rise: The Impact of the Byzantine, Polish-Lithuanian and Mongolian Empires on Muscovy

It remains unclear how many Eastern Slavs adopted Islam following the example of their Mongolian rulers in the thirteenth, fourteenth and fifteenth centuries, but one suspects that many did.[1] It is, however, more evident that Orthodox-Christian resistance developed, which was especially robust among monks. They sometimes chose to move to remote regions. While some of them preferred a solitary existence as hermits, others joined up with fellow monks and established monasteries in these faraway corners. In this way, the extent of Slavic settlement grew, especially in northern and northeastern directions from Kyiv, and striking out far beyond the Vladimir-Suzdal' region that they settled earlier. The Slavic monks encountered pagan Finno-Ugrian communities such as the Komi and Mordovian peoples in these areas, who gradually converted to Orthodoxy. Thus, even though much of what is today's central Russia was ruled by Islamic Tatars, Slavic- and Orthodox-dominated areas expanded between 1240 and 1480, the latter year being somewhat arbitrarily selected by historians as marking the end of the 'Mongol Yoke' over Muscovy.[2]

Meanwhile, most of northern Eurasia was primarily populated by a scattered patchwork of isolated communities, religiously adhering to an eclectic or idiosyncratic paganism, or to a half-hearted monotheism. For even if such communities nominally converted to Islam or Christianity, adherence to these major organized religions was often skin deep. The Russian twentieth-century philosopher Georgii Fedotov (1886–1951) observed that even in his own day the Eastern Slavs themselves remained adherents of a 'dual faith' (*dvoeverie*). Theirs was a creed that mixed pagan and Christian elements and followed a potpourri of traditions and rituals that were only half-Orthodox. Of course, even in Western Europe remnants of pre-Christian beliefs survive in modern Christianity, while historians have recognized that both Protestant and Catholic churches decided to engage in a so-called confessionalization offensive in the seventeenth century as folk or popular religion was found to be rife with superstition and riddled with customs that had little to do with officially sanctioned Christianity.

Despite the sort of dual faith of the Orthodox flock, the role of Orthodox clerics in fuelling a Russian craving to become independent from the Mongols was undeniably important. In addition, the Orthodox Church was instrumental in moving the political centre of the Eastern Slavonic world from Kyiv to Moscow. First, the see of the Eastern Slavonic metropolitan (the head of the Orthodox Church) moved from Kyiv to the central Russian town of Vladimir. A key moment in boosting the self-confidence of the rulers of Moscow was the subsequent migration of the *metropolitan*, Peter (*c.* 1260–1326), from nearby Vladimir to their city. Peter's successors as heads of the Eastern-Slavonic church stayed in Moscow.

While central Russia remained firmly under Tatar control for almost a quarter of a millennium, the northernmost segment of the Eastern Slavs lived an almost independent existence

Cathedral of the Dormition in Vladimir, central Russia.

from the Mongols: the burgeoning city states of Novgorod and Pskov belonged to an almost separate economic zone and, towards 1300, became important trading partners of the Baltic and North Sea littoral's Hanseatic League. When Mongol control began to weaken, it was Moscow, however, that emerged as the largest principality of the Russians. Novgorod rivalled it in economic importance, but was militarily feeble and proved incapable of defending itself against Moscow's attempts to bring it to heel after 1450.

The Ukrainians and Belarusians remained for a much shorter period under Tatar rule than their northeastern kin in Moscow and the cities surrounding it, such as Tver', Riazan or Vladimir. Those Ruthenians resided in what was the westernmost periphery of Mongol control after 1240, a territory that the Tatars relinquished without too much resistance, once the Grand Duchy of Lithuania began its rise under Grand Duke Gediminas (*c.* 1275–1341) in the early fourteenth century. The Ruthenian language developed separately from northern Russian after 1240; it then split into Belarusian, a language somewhat more influenced by the Lithuanian tongue, and Ukrainian, which absorbed more Polish traits. It is equally evident that late medieval Russian absorbed some Mongolian-Turkic words, such as *dengi* for money.

Even so, the transformation of an *Ur*-Eastern Slavonic into three languages was in part an autonomous process. Support for this argument can be found in the use of Chancery Slavonic as the written language of Lithuania; as a consequence, Belarusian may have been the least contaminated of the three

Remains of the wooden castle of Lithuanian Grand-Duke Gediminas.

languages that developed out of Eastern Slavonic, since Ukrainian and Russian were far more influenced by the language of their respective Polish and Tatar overlords. Certainly, the Eastern Slavonic differentiation into three languages took place at the same time as in Western Europe a language such as Dutch (itself still hard to distinguish from *Plattdeutsch* or Lower German) began to become distinct from High German, a process which had little relation to any particular imposition of foreign rule over the Low Countries. It is difficult to pinpoint the precise moment at which regional dialects become so different that they can be considered different languages, and there is no clear consensus about this among linguists (or the consensus changes over time). But, as Plokhy points out, no later than 1600 Russian, Ukrainian and Belarusian had become different languages with abundantly distinctive features.[3]

Such linguistic differentiation, though, was denied by the Imperial Russian government in the nineteenth century, when the link between language and imperial identity began to matter in a much more explicit fashion. The later Romanov regime considered Ukrainian and Belarusian peasant dialects, all the more so to deny any legitimacy to demands about claims for greater cultural and political autonomy among the Ruthenian intelligentsia. The argument of the tsars and their backers was that merely one Eastern Slavonic language (Russian or *russkii*) existed, and Russians, Ukrainians and Belarusians essentially all spoke a version of it. This common language made the Russian Empire (*Rossiiskaia imperiia*) one in which the titular nation of Russian speakers was far larger than any other, encompassing two-thirds of the total population towards 1900. Therefore, this was really a Russian, rather than a multi-ethnic, empire.

In fact, in the 1897 census ethnic Russians (then often named Great Russians, with Ukrainians being called Little Russians and Belarusians White Russians) alone amounted to a plurality, but numbered fewer than half of the total population. The Russification policies of the last two tsars would have seemed a hopeless endeavour if this reality had been accepted. Starting instead from the premise that out of a total population of 125 million more than 80 million people were Russian by including Ukrainians and Belarusians, the inculcation of a Russian identity across the empire seemed a policy no more unrealistic than the project of making peasants into Frenchmen (as Eugen Weber called it) undertaken in contemporaneous France by Jules Ferry (1832–1893) and others.[4]

But the issue of ethnocultural identity hardly played in the fifteenth or sixteenth century. For example, once eastern Ukraine was brought under the tsar's authority in 1667, many among its Polish- or Ukrainian-speaking *szlachta* (nobility) showed few qualms in petitioning to become Aleksei Mikhailovich's subjects, instead of remaining vassals of his Polish counterpart, King John Casimir (Jan II Kazimierz, 1609–1672). Such a move promised to allow these lords to continue to keep their lands and exploit their serfs who tilled it for them, rather than being expropriated and banished to Polish territory. Similarly, rulers of various Caucasian communities or German-speaking nobles in the Baltic area became Muscovite subjects without much hesitation. Their different religion and language did not stop them from switching their allegiance to the tsar. This had much to do with the weakness, or even absence, of nationalism in most of the world before the nineteenth century, but was equally rooted in this upper stratum's desire to continue to enjoy the property and privileges they had held under their previous sovereign. Similar to how other European or Asian monarchs dealt with local elites in ruling their realms, the tsars relied on these privileged castes in governing their empire, and allowed them to continue to lord it over their peasants in exchange.

Besides the struggle to escape the 'Mongol Yoke', Moscow faced both nearby rivals for its claim to the mantle of Kyiv and a growing, more distant, challenge from the mighty Polish-Lithuanian state that arose in the fourteenth century. After years of violent conflict, Moscow's competition with Tver', some 200 kilometres northwest of Moscow, ended through the deft intrigues of the Muscovite prince Ivan I (1288–1340) at the court of the northwestern Mongolian capital of Sarai on the Volga. Even though from Ivan I's time the Tatar khans began to bestow the title of grand prince on Moscow's chiefs, Moscow

Cathedral of the Resurrection in the old Russian town of Kashin in Tver' province.

was not the strongest northern Russian principality in terms of territorial size and economic strength before 1450. As said, Novgorod outstripped Moscow.

Although a slight success was scored by the Muscovite prince Dmitrii (1350–1389) with his victory over a Mongol army at Kulikovo in 1380 (a victory ballyhooed ever since as one of the greatest of Russian history, even if at the time it did not change anything politically), for another century after it Moscow's formal subjugation to the khans remained largely uncontested. The Muscovites undermined their strength through a lengthy civil war between various claimants to their principality's throne in the first half of the fifteenth century.

This infighting was all the more risky because, around the same time as Moscow descended into turmoil, the kingdom of Poland became more firmly linked to the Lithuanian grand duchy. The initial step towards this unification was the marriage between the Lithuanian ruler Wladyslaw Jagiello (Jogaila, *c.* 1360–1434) and the Polish heir Jadviga (*c.* 1373–1399) in 1385. This Union of Krewo called for the Lithuanians, the last pagans of Europe, to convert to (Western) Christianity. As a result, Wladyslaw formally ruled a country that was by far the largest in Christian Europe qua geographic size, stretching from Krakow to Kursk and from the Baltic to the Black Sea. Lithuania used Chancery Slavonic in keeping its records, as we saw, while perhaps even a majority of its population was Orthodox rather than Catholic. Eastern Slavic Smolensk may have been the largest city in Lithuania. And the Muscovite prince Vasily I (1371–1425) married a princess (Sofia, 1371–1453) of the Lithuanian ruling house.

But Poland and Lithuania remained largely separate states, merely linked through a personal union. Their loose cohesion helped Moscow escape subjugation by this potential behemoth: rather than facing Poland and Lithuania together, before the sixteenth century Muscovy usually faced the military force of Lithuania alone. And it seemed foolhardy to the Lithuanians to try to replace the still formidable Mongols in lording it over Muscovy. Meanwhile, periods of conflict between Muscovy and Lithuania alternated with periods of relative peace.

The conflict about Vasily I's succession in Muscovy was only resolved in favour of Vasily II (r. 1425–62), who had been blinded by his rivals, towards the end of the latter's life. The key figure in ending this conflict was Vasily II's son Ivan (1440–1505), the later Ivan III, who might be called the real founder of Muscovy's empire. Ivan III is one of the Russian rulers who have been awarded the title of 'Great' in hindsight. He may be more deserving of his title than either Peter I or Catherine II.

Ivan III's feats are impressive, indeed. He ended the civil war within Muscovy, married Sofia Paleologos, the niece of the last Byzantine emperor, annexed the city of Novgorod and its vast territories and faced down the Qipchak (Mongol) khans at the river Ugra in 1480. That latter event might not have been a genuine declaration of Muscovite independence, but the attempts by Tatar khans to command Russian obedience thereafter became ever weaker and ever more intermittent. Expressing Ivan III's political prowess, during his rule several of the Kremlin churches as well as the Kremlin wall were erected that survive until this day.

Ivan III was the real founding father, the true architect of Muscovy as an empire. It appears that he was the first to be occasionally called tsar, and he adopted the two-headed eagle as his symbol, emulating the coat of arms of Byzantium. He was the first to codify the laws of Muscovy in his 1497 *Sudebnik*.

And Ivan's policies, in part because of the influx of Greeks accompanying or following Sofia Paleologos, acquired a much more militant Orthodox guise. Threatened by Lithuania in the west and the various Tatar khanates in the south and southeast, Moscow's siege mentality was further cemented in his time.

The achievements of Ivan's son Vasily III (r. 1505–33) were more modest, but he consolidated Muscovy's power, recovered Smolensk and successfully held off both Lithuanians and Tatars during most of his rule. During his reign, contacts with European countries beyond Poland-Lithuania became more regular (even if the first European architects, gunners, smiths and doctors had arrived in Moscow before 1500). Charles V's envoy Sigismund von Herberstein was one of the first Europeans to report – indignantly – on the imperial ambitions of the Russian grand prince.[5] After its first publication in Latin in 1549, Herberstein's work was often translated into other European languages and it set the tone for works about Russia for a long time after. While it reflects Eurocentric surprise at the alleged lack of refinement at Moscow's court, it is also the first comprehensive text that depicts Russia as an ambitious or, indeed, pretentious power, usurping a self-proclaimed imperial title to which it had no right in European eyes. This Western effort to disparage Russia's status and significance was to continue until and beyond Peter the Great's time.

The Russian court, however, felt that it had every right to use the title of *imperator* for its ruler, as Vasily III did when he had his clerks draw up letters in Latin. After all, Moscow was now the only Orthodox state that was independent, while Vasily III's mother had been a Byzantine princess. There had always been two emperors (at least) in Christianity, so Moscow was justified in (re-)claiming the Eastern Roman imperial status for itself. Under Vasily III, the monk Filofei declared that Moscow in fact was the capital of the final true Christian state to exist before the Day of Judgement, a third and final Rome, after Italian Rome's fall to Catholic heresy and Constantinople's occupation by the Ottoman Turks.[6] Although the significance of Filofei's words may have been exaggerated by modern historians, their claim that Russians were God's chosen people did reflect the sense of embattlement prevalent in Muscovy until at least Peter the Great's time.

The already watchful collective mindset of the Russians was epitomized, as well as perverted, by Vasily's successor Ivan IV (1530–1584). Ivan has gone down in history as 'the Terrible', a not wholly accurate English translation of *Groznyi* ('awesome' in its older meaning of 'awe-inspiring' may be more apt). It is not quite clear, however, when this moniker was awarded; in West European languages the nickname may have only become fashionable towards 1700. In the Russian folk (oral) tradition, as in songs, Ivan is sometimes quite favourably remembered, possibly because whatever reign of terror he unleashed on his retainers largely bypassed the commoners (with the exception of Novgorod's citizens). Western texts published before the late seventeenth century, meanwhile, often conflated Vasily III and Ivan IV as Moscow's 'tyrants'. This appears to express Western discomfort with the absence of any evident checks on the tsar's power, such as to be found in the law courts, parliaments, city councils, noble councils, or church bodies that curbed royal power in the Western states, but was perhaps less universally dismissive as Ivan IV's later 'terrible' nickname.

Initially, Ivan IV did follow in the footsteps of his father and grandfather in further building up the Russian empire; the bad part of his reign did not quite negate the constructive first fifteen years or so that followed his official coronation as tsar in 1547. He oversaw another law codification, called a church council, and reorganized his military, as well as introducing on a large scale harquebuses (firearms) in his musketeer (*strel'tsy*) regiments. He brought order to the system of land tenure, which made noble retainers' usufruct of the soil, and its largely enserfed cultivators, dependent on their cavalry service in the army. He also began to trade overseas with the English, who docked at the mouth of the northern Dvina on the White Sea. Eventually the port of Arkhangel'sk was founded there to facilitate this burgeoning trade, in which the Dutch began to overshadow the English after 1600.

Ivan IV especially made his mark on the genesis of the Russian empire by decidedly leaving behind a strategy of merely 'gathering of the lands of Rus'' (a recreation of the Kyiv principality), which had become the prime guiding principle of Muscovite foreign policy towards 1500. Instead, Ivan conquered in the 1550s the entire shore of the Volga river south of Sviiazhsk, defeating two of the smaller khanates, those of Kazan and Astrakhan, which had succeeded the once united western Mongolian khanate of the Golden Horde. Ivan IV could thus persuasively claim that he was the legitimate successor to the Tatar khans by right of conquest, a khan as well as a tsar. By 1560, Ivan IV's realm's extent surpassed that of the Polish-Lithuanians, and was easily the largest in Europe in size, albeit not in population numbers.

But then Ivan IV overestimated his country's strength. Soon after the capture of Astrakhan in 1556, the tsar decided to embark on a westward campaign to subjugate the Livonian state, successor to the principalities established by the Teutonic (German) Knights in the Baltic region in the thirteenth century.

The knights declared fealty to the Polish king and what at first promised to be an easy conquest descended into a protracted war. The Livonian Wars, which mainly pitted Muscovites against Polish-Lithuanian forces, lasted from 1558 to 1583, and ended with a clear Russian defeat. Long before the Poles were victorious, the war's toll added to other calamities that were causing havoc in Russia. Adverse climatic circumstances (the first signs of the Mini Ice Age) caused severe famines in 1560s and 1570s Muscovy, while the incidence and intensity of epidemic diseases concomitantly increased. The devastation was depicted in a travel account by the English envoy Giles Fletcher (*c.* 1549–1611), who encountered many depopulated villages when travelling through northern Muscovy in the 1580s.[7] By the early 1560s, Ivan began to suspect that plots against him undermined his fight against Poland. Rumours swirled around the court that his first wife, Anastasia Romanovna Zakhar'ina-Iur'eva (1530–1560), had been poisoned. In 1564, one of Ivan's most competent military commanders, Prince Andrei Kurbskii (1528–1583), on campaign in the Baltic, switched to the Polish side. A shocked and depressed Ivan went into voluntary internal exile and then, after his subjects begged him to return to Moscow, unleashed a reign of terror (*oprichnina*, implemented by so-called *oprichnik*s) to rid himself of any suspected foes. This seven-year-long bloodbath killed numerous high-ranking nobles (the *boyar*s) and eventually even cost the head of the Russian church, Metropolitan Filipp II (1507–1569), his life.

The biggest instance of savagery occurred in Novgorod in 1570, which was sacked by the *oprichnik*s on accusations (not entirely groundless) of the town having sought to switch sides and ally with Poland; thousands of Novgorodians were killed, while many others were deported. Although Ivan III had already reduced Novgorod's economic prosperity and general significance, Ivan IV truly turned it into a secondary city by his actions. It remained significant as a border town and administrative centre through which some foreign trade was conducted, but it never recovered its medieval significance as a leading Eastern Slavonic city that was a valued part of the Hanseatic League.

Ivan IV's purges did not change Russian fortunes in the Livonian Wars. What was possibly worse than the military setback in the west was a Crimean-Tatar raid in 1571 that laid waste to Moscow's environs and caused a fire that burned most of the wooden city down, killing many. The Tatars captured thousands of Muscovites who they took with them to Crimea. Some were ransomed, but most were sold on the Black Sea slave markets. Ivan then abolished the *oprichnik*s, blaming them for failing to stop the Tatar raiders. Until his death more than a decade later, the tsar moved in and out of psychotic episodes – in one of which he killed his oldest son.

Thus towards 1580 the Russian claim to imperial status had been strongly undermined. Ultimately, Muscovy had failed to match the power of Poland-Lithuania, which in 1568 concluded the Union of Lublin, establishing narrower ties between the two parts that made up the Rzeczpospolita, the Polish-Lithuanian Commonwealth. Neither could Muscovy deal with the Crimean Tatars yet. The Time of Troubles of the early seventeenth century might have put the nail in the coffin of this wannabe empire, but somehow it did not. Even in Ivan's dark final days, some indication hinting at a possible reinvigoration could be found in the crossing of the Ural mountains and the conquest of the (western) Siberian khanate by Cossacks in Russian service. And although Fyodor 1's rule (1584–98) did little to stave off the catastrophe that unfolded after 1600, it did witness the establishment of a Russian patriarchate in 1589, elevating Moscow's status as a centre of Orthodoxy. The head of the Russian church was now formally equal to the five other patriarchs of the Orthodox Church. Besides boosting Russia's standing in the Orthodox world, this promotion strengthened Muscovite claims to its right to rule over the Orthodox believers of Eastern Europe.

7
Troubles

Just after 1600 the very existence of Muscovy was challenged. Already devastated by the fruitless wars of Ivan IV and the harsh effects of a cooling climate, not long after Fyodor's death true catastrophe descended on Russia. Fyodor had died without issue, and the only possible relative who could have succeeded him, Dmitrii, a son of Ivan IV's seventh marriage, had died as a young boy under mysterious circumstances in 1591. The official cause of death, according to an official investigation by a leading *boyar*, Vasily Shuisky (1552–1612), was that the ten-year-old had fallen on his own sword while playing, perhaps in an epileptic fit. But Dmitrii's death seemed a bit too convenient in benefiting Tsar Fyodor's brother-in-law and main advisor, Boris Godunov (1551–1605), a former *oprichnik*. Still, Dmitrii's rights to the throne were dubious at least, as the Russian Orthodox Church's canonical law did not recognize more than three marriages. Therefore, whereas Dmitrii's death has often been depicted as orchestrated by Boris Godunov, it remains opaque whether or not Boris, or Vasily Shuisky, who was then his ally, had anything to do with it.

Muscovy's swift descent into chaos after 1600 shows a fundamental weakness that plagues absolutist or autocratic regimes. As long as powerful monarchs lead them and avoid crises, they usually survive. But if the succession to the throne

Church of St Dmitrii on the Blood in Uglich, built on the site where a body believed to be that of Tsarevich Dmitrii Ioannovich was found in 1591.

is in question, as had also occurred in Muscovy during the first half of the fifteenth century, or a mentally impaired person or child succeeds because of laws of inheritance, as was to occur in 1676, 1682 and 1727, trouble is bound to ensue. And, of course, even relatively competent rulers may be challenged in times of famine, war or epidemics. Both a contested succession and a deep economic crisis befell Muscovy around 1600. This disaster had such severe consequences that for a brief period from 1610 to 1613 Muscovy did in fact cease to exist as an independent state, as no tsar was recognized by any significant group of stakeholders. Nor did the Russian Church have a patriarch from 1612 to 1619.

Fyodor I was at best a weak monarch. A very pious man, he was possibly not quite in his right mind; indeed, some of his behaviour reminds one of that of a holy fool (*iurod'*), an itinerant soothsaying character who was revered in the Russian Orthodox tradition. On the eve of his death, Ivan IV had ordered Boris Godunov, Ivan Shuisky (a cousin of Vasily) and Fyodor Nikitich Romanov (1553–1633), a nephew of Ivan IV's first wife, to lead a regency council that could rule in Fyodor's name. Godunov was the senior partner in this regency and ultimately manoeuvred himself into the position of the tsar's favourite councillor. When Fyodor died in 1598, Godunov seemed to be the only logical candidate to succeed him. A meeting of some of the country's most important secular and religious leaders duly proclaimed Godunov tsar.

Perhaps Tsar Boris Godunov might have fit the bill of a strong monarch, but he did not rule long enough to become one, while he lacked the good fortune to escape a severe crisis. Further failed harvests caused an enormous famine to break out by 1603, and, while the tsar had been prudent enough to store grain in granaries, demand far outstripped supply. The foundations of the Muscovite Empire began to shake. To ensure that enough crop tillage and animal husbandry were conducted on noble lands to enable the noble army to go on campaign, enserfment of the peasantry had become widespread during the second half of the sixteenth century. After 1600, desperate people fled the lands to which the law had tied them, because they could no longer meet their obligations as serfs. Some went to inhospitable and remote areas towards the Arctic Circle, while others tried to join the freebooting Cossacks in the southern borderlands. Noble warriors were thus deprived of the means needed to fight in the tsar's army.

Unable to turn the tide of suffering, Boris Godunov received the blame for much of the misery. The leading *boyar*s whom he had sidetracked in the 1590s began to stir. By 1604 Muscovy was engaged in an undeclared war with the armed forces of someone who proclaimed himself to be Dmitrii, the son of Ivan IV, who apparently had not died in 1591. It seemed obvious that this was a pretender who lied about his identity, but the problem was that 'Dmitrii' (called False Dmitrii, *Lzhedmitrii*, in most historiography) garnered the support of Polish-Lithuanian magnates, the Catholic Church, and eventually the Polish royal house. All saw an opportunity to increase their power and wealth in the escalating mayhem that engulfed Muscovy.

By this time, the Catholic Counterreformation was picking up steam in the Polish Commonwealth, which had previously been a polity in which a number of religions were tolerated. At least since the 1570s, however, Jesuits had been chipping away at this lenience. One of the ways in which they furthered the Catholic cause was by convincing a considerable part of the Ruthenian Orthodox hierarchy in Ukraine and Belarus to submit to the pope in Rome, while promising to leave almost every other Orthodox tradition in place, including priestly marriage! This Union of Brest of 1596 between the Ruthenian Orthodox Church and the Roman Catholic Church upset both traditionally minded Ukrainian and Belarusian clergy and believers and the Muscovite government and Russian Orthodox Church.

In 1604 it seemed to many of the Orthodox stalwarts that the Counterreformatory crusade arrived on Muscovite soil in the guise of the pretender Dmitrii and his small army. One town after the next in the western borderlands surrendered to them without much resistance, as loyalty to Boris Godunov appeared to be halting at best and the army had been weakened through rural depopulation. The False Dmitrii's cause was then incomparably aided by the death of Godunov in April 1605. Tsar Boris had named his son Fyodor (1589–1605) as his successor, but few in Moscow were willing to serve this teenager. The *boyars* with whom Boris Godunov had quarrelled parlayed with the pretender and made sure that a transfer of power occurred without further combat: Fyodor II was killed and Dmitrii proclaimed tsar in Moscow in June 1605.

The problem for the new tsar was that he was by no means the unanimous candidate of all rivalling court factions, with the senior Orthodox clergy especially hostile because Dmitrii (who seems to have been raised Orthodox) had converted to Catholicism in Poland in 1604. It is likely as well that some of the *boyars* were wary of Dmitrii as he was supported by numerous Cossacks. Their very presence in Moscow was a challenge to the social hierarchy, for Cossacks were either themselves refugee serfs, or descendants of those who had fled serfdom.

Before a year was over after he had been welcomed as tsar, Dmitrii faced key opponents of his rule lined up in an alliance against him. The catalyst for his fall was his marriage to the daughter of his Polish sponsor, Marina Mniszech, who, unlike Dmitrii who had returned to the Orthodox fold to get crowned, refused to become an Orthodox believer. Dmitrii's soldiers, Catholic and Protestant alike, had been defiling Muscovite churches as the tsar had permitted them to pray in Orthodox churches, which was anathema to Russian Orthodox beliefs. The hostility towards Dmitrii was now bundled by none other than Vasily Shuisky, the main investigator into the real Dmitrii's death in Uglich in 1591. Dmitrii was massacred by a mob led by a number of *boyars* in May 1606.

Troubles

But Vasily Shuisky, who was now proclaimed Tsar Vasily IV, faced the same problems his predecessors had encountered during their short reigns. The economic crisis was by no means over, and Muscovy was now concomitantly engaged in a war with Poland-Lithuania. Nor was Shuisky popular among all Russian stakeholders. Meanwhile, in the borderlands Cossacks remained restless, and a genuine popular army made up of Cossacks, serfs and lower nobility under Ivan Bolotnikov (1565–1608) marched on Moscow in 1606. This social rebellion went too far for the nobles in the end and they temporarily rallied behind Vasily IV. But even before Bolotnikov's defeat, another pretender, known to history as False Dmitrii II, had appeared. He managed to gain the support of the Lithuanians and Poles, and, bizarrely, was recognized by Marina Mniszech as her husband. But even though this pretender camped out mere miles from Moscow, he and his forces never gained entrance to the city.

At what seemed to be a most propitious moment, the Polish king Sigismund Wasa (1566–1632) decided that it was time to take ownership over the anti-Shuisky forces, ignoring the second pretender: after more than two centuries, it seemed the Polish(-Lithuanian)-Muscovite conflict would be settled by a Polish triumph. Before this succession could be ratified, meanwhile, the second impostor was forced to flee when attacked by an army of soldiers loyal to Mikhail Skopin-Shuisky (1586–1610; Vasily IV's distant cousin) reinforced by Swedish allies.

In the autumn of 1609, Polish troops began to besiege Smolensk; they moved deeper into Muscovite territory in the spring of 1610 and provoked another rebellion against the tsar in Moscow. Vasily IV abdicated and was ultimately handed over to the Poles; he died in Polish captivity. The Poles were now masters of Moscow: the history of Muscovy, it appeared, had come to an end. But, as during their previous backing of the first False Dmitrii, the Poles overplayed their hand. Not all Muscovites recognized Polish sovereignty, particularly because of the Western Christian beliefs of the Kremlin's occupiers. Most crucially, the Russian Orthodox Church, whose Patriarch Germogen (1530–1612) was eventually confined by the Poles to a monastery and subsequently killed, stubbornly refused to recognize the Polish prince Wladyslaw (1595–1648), the son of King Sigismund, as tsar. In addition, Polish military control over much of Russia was tentative. Vasily Shuisky's Swedish allies, who had fought against the second False Dmitrii, had set out on their own and occupied much of northwestern Russia, unwilling to submit to the Poles in Moscow. Finally, the Cossacks in various parts remained restless.

A Muscovite rally could therefore gain momentum and an army of Russian commoners, Cossacks and *boyar*s forced the Poles to surrender the Kremlin after a siege. In early 1613 a meeting of representatives of Russian nobles, clergy and townspeople elected a tsar who did prove to have staying power, Mikhail Romanov (1596–1645), whose great-aunt had been the first wife of Ivan IV. Even if new pretenders challenged the young monarch, Mikhail and his advisors showed a unity of purpose, and received the full backing of the Orthodox Church. The church's representatives subsequently, in 1619, elected Mikhail's father Fyodor Nikitich, who had been forced to become a monk by Godunov and taken the name of Filaret, as patriarch. Filaret had been apprehended by the Poles in 1609, and spent years in Polish captivity. He was only released under the terms of the Treaty of Deulino of 1618, which proclaimed a Polish-Muscovite truce. Meanwhile, the war with Sweden lasted until the 1617

Treaty of Stolbovo. In order to end the conflict in both cases, Muscovy had to accept significant territorial losses along its borders, but the wars that continued after Mikhail's elevation to tsar seem to have had the positive effect of galvanizing Russian unity in the face of those foreign foes.

It would be hard to measure how far the 1613 election of Mikhail Romanov confirms that Muscovy was in reality far from an empire led by an autocrat, but rather one led by a government in which the tsar ruled by consent. Was early Romanov Russia an autocracy in name rather than in fact, based on a tacit agreement by which all the stakeholders, such as the *boyar*s, *dvor'iane* (gentry), bishops and other high clergy, high-level bureaucrats and merchants agreed to uphold a facade that made it seem that the tsar was all-powerful?[1] Two things might be worth pondering in considering this question. In the first place, one may recognize a possible parallel with the Putin regime in today's Russia. While a superficial look at Vladimir Putin's leadership of Russia leads many observers to conclude that he is well-nigh an all-powerful dictator, others have convincingly suggested that he is presented as such in the interest of powerful circles in today's Russia. That is not to say that Putin is a mere straw man (neither was Mikhail Romanov), but that, while behaving like an autocrat in public, he needs to carefully consider the interests of many stakeholders in making his decisions.

Second, some of the puzzling moves made by Peter the Great around 1700 make better sense if one views his predecessors as autocrats in name more than in fact. Although his empire's modernization, especially in military terms, was foremost on his agenda, Peter also appears to have tried to curtail the power of those who had meddled (behind the scenes) in the previous reigns: church leaders and the *boyar*s who cherished old-fashioned cultural traditions and political customs were demoted and diminished; indeed, Peter did away with some traditional institutions cramping his style, such as the patriarchate and the powerful musketeer force of the *strel'tsy*. By the time of his death, Peter was far freer to act as he saw fit, as a genuine autocrat, than when he began his offensive a quarter of a century earlier. And he had been formally proclaimed *imperator*.

8

From Mikhail to Peter: Composite Empire and Middle Ground

Given the utter state of decomposition in which it was mired around 1610, Romanov Muscovy's recovery in the later 1610s and across the 1620s appears well-nigh astonishing. The question of how this occurred deserves more attention from historians, but one can at least surmise that the ruin was not as severe as it appeared. This hypothesis may remain hard to verify even if investigated more closely: as the mayhem destroyed many records, sufficient sources seem to be lacking, making it difficult to come to a definitive conclusion.[1] Nonetheless, a few points deserve consideration in this matter.

First, it might be proposed that the Romanovs fell back on a manner of organizing the defence of their realm in a tried-and-true fashion.[2] Serfdom's roots in Muscovy dated back to the late fifteenth century, when the freedom of movement of peasants was curtailed to ensure that crops, especially grain and hay, were grown and dairy or meat was produced to feed the men and horses of the mounted cavalry that fought the Muscovite grand duke's wars. Peasants tended to move away from lords who made them give up their surplus to sustain their military exploits, but if they absconded in significant numbers the army could not go on campaign. Eventually, after the 1550s, when population numbers notably dropped through failed

Muscovy-Russia in the 17th century.

harvests, warfare and disease, the limited peasant freedom to move elsewhere was further reduced. Peasants were formally tied to the land they tilled. Concomitantly, since Ivan IV's rule at least, few of the Russian gentry (*dvor'iane*) were allowed to hold land (and the peasants who worked it) in full ownership without rendering military service for its use (so-called conditional tenure). Around this time, a similar process of enserfment took place across Europe east of the Elbe river, even if its cause may not always have been the same. In the Rzeczpospolita, for example, the surplus grain was so plentiful that it not merely allowed the local nobles (*szlachta*) to go to war, but could be exported in great amounts. In Muscovy, grain harvests were not consistently ample enough to sustain a regular sale of the surplus to foreign merchants.

In the Troubles, peasants' anger at enserfment found expression, but not to the degree that it stopped the Muscovite government after 1613 from returning to its own traditions (and those of its neighbours) of outfitting its military through unfree labour. It seemed to make sense to use this system, especially because much of the army consisted of mounted troops in an economy in which the use of money was still far from universal. Government and nobles understood that peasants might protest against their plight through flight or rebellion, but no clear alternative offered itself to sustain the army. Because population numbers remained low and opportunities to seek one's luck elsewhere were tempting thanks to the vast size of Russia, peasants were once again, after the Time of Troubles, tied to the land. This process reached its culmination in 1649, when the law code (*Ulozhenie*) decreed that all those who worked the land were to remain serfs in perpetuity. The occasional revolt seemed an acceptable price to pay.

Serfdom had the additional advantage that the state could collect taxes (often paid in kind to the lords) much more easily from a stationary population. Taxes needed to be raised by the government because the state bureaucracy and special military units, such as the *strel'tsy*, or projects, such as the fortified border in the south, needed to be supported as well as the cavalry and infantry units that went on campaign. Gradually, more money came into circulation on the seventeenth-century Russian market, making the practice of the collection and distribution of taxes slightly less cumbersome. Even if the army was ever more professionalized, serfdom remained in force in much of Russia, Belarus and Ukraine until 1861; the gentry formed the bulk of the army's officer corps long after its obligation to serve the empire was abolished in 1762.

The recovery was also swift, perhaps, because it was a return to a rather basic standard of living. Seventeenth-century Western observers frequently noted the remarkable agility with which the Muscovites could restore parts of their largely wooden city after fire burned down their houses. New wooden buildings went up in a day. (The Kremlin, made of brick and stone, escaped extensive destruction.) Flexibility or adaptability, this suggests, may have been a trait particularly strongly developed among the Muscovites. In the countryside, houses, stables and huts were also made of wood, and even in peaceful times might thus fall prey to fire, which called for a similarly defiant attitude in the face of hardship among villagers. During the Troubles, many peasants may have set up shop elsewhere if the battling came too close, following time-honoured traditions. That the Romanovs reiterated the sixteenth-century decrees forbidding the peasants to move hints at a widespread inclination to migrate on the part of the serfs, rather than stubbornly 'sinking roots' in the same spot. In addition, some of the bureaucrats who ran the government administration seem to have stayed in place throughout the entire era, starting their careers under Boris Godunov and ending up clerks for Tsar Mikhail Romanov. Key parts of the government apparatus may have continued to function throughout the Time of Troubles without long-term interruption.

But it may have played a role as well that Russia's government as such was extremely small. As elsewhere in Europe, most revenue went to the military. Even that military was still paid in part in kind by the government, and had in some measure to survive off the proceeds of the labour of its serfs. Cash was scarce in Russia in the first decades of the seventeenth century, according to Jarmo Kotilaine.[3] And the central government apparatus, while comparatively large by European standards, consisted of only a few hundred clerks. The country probably had fewer than 10 million inhabitants in 1613, of whom many remained almost wholly out of the government's reach and therefore did not contribute anything to government income. By 1650, population density was less than one person per square mile, if Siberia is included in this calculation.[4] All of this helps us to understand why the devastation of the Time of Troubles may have been more apparent than real: it was not all that difficult to resurrect this small and limited machinery of state, or to rekindle an economy that was not especially complex.

Another characteristic trait of early modern empires such as Muscovite Russia should be taken into account: the actual power of the tsar outside of Moscow and its immediate surroundings was limited. We saw how the tsar had to rely on local governors (*voevody*) and their senior bureaucrats (*d'iaky*) to enforce his power. They did so usually from the larger towns that dotted the European-Russian and Siberian landscape. Muscle was provided by – usually fairly small – units of *strel'tsy*, or by Cossacks, as in Siberia. The only real check the tsar had on these satraps and their civilian and military staff was the use of a rotation system, which had most of the *voevody* stay no longer than three years in one place. Furthermore, any overly independent streak was mitigated by the fact that the governors were recruited from the leading *boyar* families, who preferred to remain on good terms with the tsar in order to continue to enjoy the imperial spoils.

The governors and their officials and soldiery, however, needed to use caution in exerting power in the tsar's name, for, given the vast distances, military assistance from Moscow could hardly be rendered immediately in cases of popular unrest. Local officials usually avoided behaving overly arbitrarily, as they could ill afford to anger the population of their fief given their own limited and often inadequate military strength in the face of revolts, which were endemic throughout the entire early modern period. In Orthodox regions, the Church (and the noble servitors who served in the military) aided the secular authorities by imploring patience, loyalty and deference to the tsar's rule among their flock, but in non-Orthodox areas it could become exceedingly difficult to keep the peace when the governors were suspected of extracting fees that were too high, or of collecting taxes and tribute at an amount seen as unjust. The *strel'tsy* could only do so much at such moments. Thus, as has been cogently argued by Matthew Romaniello and Mikhail Khodarkovsky, Muscovy was a composite empire; in some borderlands, indeed, the non-Russian indigenous population saw Russians as their partners or allies, rather than their rulers.[5] Bashkirs, Nogais and others still met Russians on a Middle Ground, similar to that in contemporary North America described by Richard White.[6] The Stepan Razin rebellion of 1670–71, which set most of the Volga littoral aflame, especially proved how delicate the empire's condition was. In some places, of course, bullying might work, as it did across much of Siberia. But this had to do with the weakness of those subjected to state-sponsored violence. The Siberian communities were small and few communicated with each other, which made the conclusion of any alliance among them a remote possibility. They also lacked the firearms wielded by the Russians.

It must be emphasized, though, that the tsar's flimsy hold on his country was the norm in this era for potentates. The Mughal rulers of South Asia, for example, could never quite establish control over their southern borderlands, and Aurangzeb (1618–1707) may have set their power on an irreversible decline by over-extending southwards. In Iran, as Rudi Matthee suggests, the shah's rule in regions far away from Isfahan was weak.[7] Even Louis XIV, ruling relatively compact France, had little control over the more remote areas of his kingdom.[8]

If we take into account such limitations, though, it can be proposed that Muscovy regained its former (relative) strength rather quickly.[9] This allowed in the course of the 1620s for the tsar and his father, Patriarch Filaret, to contemplate retrieving the territories lost to Poland and Sweden in the treaties of 1617 and 1618. The building of the southern fortification lines to keep out the Tatars resumed as well. In the 1680s and 1690s, the Russians even took the offensive against the Crimean Tatars, but any permanent advantage against them was gained only after Peter the Great's death, not least because the Tatars were backed by the mighty Ottoman Turks. Of the three key Russian opponents – Ottoman Turks and Tatars; Poles and Lithuanians; and Swedes – Poland proved the weakest, in part because it was often rent asunder by domestic strife. Before the 1680s, Poland was the usual target of the tsars' military campaigning.

The rivalry with Poland was long-standing, of course, while that with Sweden was relatively new. Sweden displayed imperial ambitions throughout much of the seventeenth century. The Swedes were involved in an effort of sorts to make the Baltic Sea into a Swedish lake, a strategy that gained renewed momentum under King Gustavus Adolphus (r. 1611–32). Sweden stood in Russia's way, having definitively ended the Muscovite attempt to have a port on the Baltic Sea by occupying its eastern shores during the Troubles. In winter, the Baltic Sea was frozen for a much shorter time than the White Sea, and an outlet there would bring Muscovy much closer to the bustling ports of Amsterdam, Hamburg, Bremen and London, from which strategic goods such as firearms and luxury commodities that were in high demand originated, not least at the tsar's court. The Russians had temporarily held Narva in the Livonian wars, while even afterwards they held on to adjacent Ivangorod, only to ultimately lose it in 1612. In other words, Peter the Great was not original in his famed search for a 'window on the West'. He was just more successful than his father or grandfather in fighting the Swedes, and, even while still in the midst of war with them in 1703, ordered the building of St Petersburg on formerly Swedish land.

Rather than challenging a rising Sweden, though, Tsar Mikhail Romanov and Patriarch Filaret set their sights on the country that had brought Muscovy the most grief in the Troubles: Poland-Lithuania. While they appear to have had a fairly good understanding of how the art of war was changing in significant ways on the contemporary battlefields of the Low Countries and the Holy Roman Empire, the Russian army's expanded use of modern weapons, such as more sophisticated muskets, and mercenary skill, proved to be insufficient to beat the Poles in the Smolensk War (1632–4). Indeed, many of the mercenaries hired in continental Western Europe and Great Britain fled this war's battlefields once their regular pay was no longer forthcoming. Even before that, communication between Russian commanders and troops and foreign hirelings had been poor. The death of the virulently anti-Polish Filaret in 1633 allowed the Russians to admit that nothing could be gained from prolonging a war for which they were not ready.

After his father's death, Mikhail proved gun-shy, or, perhaps, wisely prudent. In 1637 Cossacks seized the Crimean Tatar stronghold of Azov, and offered the fortress to the tsar in exchange for his military support against any Tatar and Ottoman attempts to recover it. After much hesitation and a discussion with all stakeholders in Moscow, Mikhail definitively rejected the offer. Together with his advisors, the tsar decided that his country was by no means prepared to take on the mighty Ottoman Empire. The first lasting Russian successes against Ottoman forces were only achieved a century later.

But Mikhail's son Aleksei (r. 1645–76) was more successful in fighting Poland, while his grandson Peter (r. 1682–1725) not only crippled Poland, but forced Sweden to abandon the eastern littoral of the Baltic. Aleksei was less cautious than his father, and willing to take calculated risks. But he prepared carefully for his offensive against Poland-Lithuania. He succeeded his father while still a teenager and almost immediately faced domestic unrest. The volatile mood in Moscow was only calmed by another assembly of the representatives of all of Muscovy's non-enserfed population, which enacted a law code (*Ulozhenie*) that was to be in force for the next six generations. In 1650 the last rebellious eruptions ended and Aleksei could seriously ready his country for war.

Like his father, he used foreign mercenaries, but his key move was to reorganize and retrain his army into 'new formation regiments', mainly composed of Russians who fought in a more European style. Western-made arms were imported by the tens of thousands through Arkhangel'sk in the early 1650s, even if Muscovite troops were also beginning to be supplemented by a growing domestic arms industry that had been set up by Dutchmen. A convenient *casus belli* was found in Polish defeats of rebellious Ukrainian Cossacks, who since 1648 had tried to defy the king. Although the causes of the Cossack *ataman* (chief) Bohdan Khmel'nits'kii's uprising were in part purely personal, the Cossacks 'beyond the [Dnipro] rapids' (*Zaporizhiya*, or, in Russian, *Zaporozhe*) did increasingly resent the greater control Warsaw was trying to impose on them and the continuing attempt to have Ukrainians join the Orthodox Uniate Church, which since 1596 had recognized the pope as its head. This religious issue, too, helped Aleksei rally the Russians behind him. In this policy, he was supported by his wilful patriarch, Nikon (1605–1681), who had been elected in 1652.

Nikon aligned the Russian Orthodox Church's liturgy with the practices of the Greek Orthodox mother church, and thus the Ukrainian Orthodox Church, using the aid of Ukrainian clergymen in this effort. Whereas this made it easier for *ataman*

Khmel'nits'kii to sign the 1654 Treaty of Pereiaslavl' with Aleksei, Nikon's reforms caused an uproar within the Russian Church. Many among clergy and faithful believed that Nikon was corrupting the sacred traditions of the uniquely Russian creed and was thus an instrument of evil forces. They separated themselves from the main church, becoming known in English as the Old Believers (*staroobriadtsy* in Russian, literally meaning 'Old Ritualists').[10] Once their protest was condemned by the Moscow Church Council of 1666–7, their attitude became uncompromising: a number of Old Believer communities preferred setting themselves alight in their wooden houses of worship rather than submitting to Moscow's secular and spiritual rule.

The Treaty of Pereiaslavl' is an almost perfect expression of Richard White's Middle Ground, or of the contested interpretation of a *shert'* as outlined by Mikhail Khodarkovsky. The Russians interpreted the agreement as a fulsome submission by the Ukrainian Cossacks to the tsar's rule. Khmel'nits'kii and his followers believed they had concluded an alliance with a mere token acknowledgement that Muscovy was its senior partner.

The problem with the Ukrainian interpretation of the Pereiaslavl' Treaty was that the Cossacks were hardly equal military partners of the Muscovites. Khmel'nits'kii's followers had been forced on the defensive, and the war with Poland was increasingly conducted by the superior fighting force that by the mid-1650s was the Muscovite army. The Ukrainian Cossacks reverted to a role as auxiliaries in the course of the war. In addition, Khmel'nits'kii died in 1657, which caused a succession crisis that in Russian eyes further diminished the value of their Ukrainian-Cossack allies. Therefore, when the

Truce of Andrusovo ended the Thirteen Years War (1654–67), its terms seemed to describe eastern Ukraine as a Russian fief rather than an independent polity. Under the terms of this Polish-Russian agreement, Moscow was given the rule over Kyiv for twenty years as well, after which the treaty was to be renegotiated. When this occurred, a year early in 1686, Kyiv was definitively handed over to Russia.

Pereiaslavl' and Andrusovo firmly underlined Muscovy's long-standing claims to be the legitimate heir of Kyivan Rus'. Not only was the head of the Orthodox Church already residing in Moscow, but after 1667 Kyiv itself fell under the tsar's rule. However, only eastern Ukraine, the territory east of the Dnipro (Dnepr) river, was Russian ruled; western Ukraine remained for more than a hundred years under Polish rule.[11] Indeed, the westernmost part of what is now Ukraine (the regions of L'viv and Uzhhorod) *never* became a part of Imperial Russia. Only in Soviet times, after the Second World War, were these territories added to the Ukrainian Socialist Soviet Republic. They have remained the least Russophile parts of Ukraine. Be that as it may, the mid-seventeenth century was the moment when Russia laid claim to Ukraine, a claim that it has never wholly rescinded.

While Aleksei's realm thus expanded in size in a southwestern direction, the tsar also made clear that he would not tolerate a type of co-rule with the patriarch in the manner of his father and grandfather during the 1620s. Nikon had been appointed as caretaker of the government when Aleksei went personally on military campaign in 1654. Serving as the tsar's deputy in Moscow fed into Nikon's sense of his own importance. He began to consider himself as the tsar's equal, which led to Aleksei berating him. A miffed Nikon went into self-imposed exile, but even if Aleksei was a very pious man, he refused to bow to the head of his church by begging Nikon to come back to Moscow. Eventually, the Church Council that condemned the Old Believers also deposed Nikon as patriarch in 1666. Aleksei's dressing down of Nikon set the table, once more, for his son Peter's actions. Doing away with the patriarchate altogether in 1721, Peter became a *caesaropapist* in the style of Constantine the Great (Roman emperor, *r*. 306–37). As spiritual-cum-secular leader, the tsar's authority over his subjects grew, and his people called him *tsar'-batiushka*, or 'tsar-little father', venerated as an almost semi-divine deputy of the great father in heaven. Moscow's patriarch, who was in place only from 1589 to 1700, never acquired such an aura.

Raison d'état, reason of state, very much informed Aleksei's actions as tsar. Although his father's support for an attempt at launching a navy to cruise on the Caspian Sea had not born fruit, Aleksei resumed the effort. Not far from Moscow, a sail-ship and several auxiliary ships were constructed at enormous expense, which were then hauled down the Oka and Volga rivers towards Astrakhan in 1669. The *Oryol* (*Eagle*) never set sail because it was captured by Razin's Cossacks, but one of the Dutch crew, who fled the Cossacks and managed to return to Moscow, crucially refurbished a vessel, the *botik*, for the young Peter the Great two decades later.[12] This truly began the story of Russia as a maritime power, as the small sail-boat fired Peter's imagination.

In the course of the seventeenth century, Russia's economy began to modernize and catch up with the more sophisticated and diversified economies of the European states to its west. Aleksei's shipbuilding project coincided with the imposition of higher tariffs on Western commodities imported through

Arkhangel'sk. News from Europe and elsewhere became much more regularly available to the court through the establishment of a regular postal service with the West. This growing stream of information stimulated trade as well. Considerable prospecting was conducted on both sides of the Urals in Aleksei's reign, which led to the opening of a variety of mining enterprises, especially of pig iron. Iron fed the growing arms manufactories. Economically, by the mid-1670s Russia was far more prosperous than ever before; even serious epidemics, as during the early stages of the Thirteen Years War, hardly dented this progress.

When Aleksei suddenly died in early 1676, he was parlaying with a Dutch embassy about the conclusion of a grand alliance that would include Prussia, the Dutch Republic and Denmark, to fight Sweden and France. His death halted this effort, but it is clear that by that time Muscovy was no longer considered an exotic country beyond the confines of Europe proper. It was now included in an early version of the 'Concert of Europe', among which a delicate balance of power was maintained. Russia was ruled by minors (for all intents and purposes) from 1676 to 1689, which made it sit out the early stages of another grand battle of Christian Europe with the Ottoman Empire that saw Vienna besieged in 1683. But after ending his half-sister's regency in 1689, Peter began to prepare for a war that would make Russia once and for all into one of Europe's great powers, joining the ranks of such behemoths as France and Britain.

At times Tsar Peter knew how to draw back when faced with poor odds, but at other times he got carried away and became dizzy with success, which in the end lessened the spoils of his victories. In his initial military campaigns, which

The first Russian naval vessel, the *botik* of Tsar Peter the Great.

saw him take the field against the Crimean Tatars, he had better luck than his half-sister's favourite, Vasily Golitsyn (1643–1714). With the aid of a considerable naval squadron, Azov was captured in 1696. Peter, who had already visited Arkhangel'sk and even earlier learned how to sail on lakes near Moscow on the *botik* and other vessels, then decided that he needed personally to learn from the best shipmasters. Thus, formally incognito, the 25-year-old tsar travelled to Western Europe to study shipbuilding in Amsterdam and London in 1697 and 1698. He additionally planned both to soak up the culture of the most advanced maritime empires of his day and to investigate diplomatic scenarios to attempt to dislodge Sweden through alliances with other European states, or, indeed, to reinvigorate the Holy Alliance that had taken on the Turks since 1683, but was beginning to lose momentum. William III, leader of both the Dutch Republic and Great Britain, while welcoming the tsar, proved non-committal. The king-stadholder's main adversary was France, which had set its sights on a Spanish inheritance that included what is modern-day Belgium; William saw neither Sweden nor the Ottoman Empire as an opponent. Peter did personally help to build a large, long-distance sailship on the wharves of the Dutch East India Company in Amsterdam, but in doing so found further confirmation that English shipwrights were more advanced than the Dutch. On his tour, he and his retinue hired hundreds of experts (mainly artisans) to work in Russia to help modernize the country further. And Peter fed his interest in science through his visits to Dutch curiosity cabinets, the Royal Observatory and the Royal Society.

From what he saw in Western Europe, Peter concluded that his country needed to undergo a broad technological modernization to become one of Europe's Great Powers. A lasting escape from the stranglehold of Sweden, Poland and the Turks, who blocked Russia from acquiring ports on the Baltic and Black Seas, could not be accomplished simply through traditional military campaigns. Dwarfing them economically was equally important, as it would allow for the build-up and maintenance of overwhelming military force, securing long-term hegemony. Ports seemed essential, for the affluence of the European maritime powers and the cornucopia of goods that they traded were evidently linked to their enormous merchant marine and navies. If Russia was to become a dominant force in Europe and the world, it needed to have a seafaring fleet and ports that were not encumbered by ice for more than half the year.

But Peter was impatient, in stark contrast to his contemporary King Frederick William (r. 1713–40) of Prussia, who spent his rule husbanding his country's military strength, never to use it in any major war. This prudence stood his son Frederick the Great (r. 1740–86) in good stead when he embarked on his project to make Prussia into a great power in Europe. Compared to Frederick William's prudence, it seems that Peter probably wanted too much too soon. It proved overly ambitious both to modernize his country and to fight conclusive wars that would get rid of its long-standing rivals in short order. In 1700, allied with Denmark and Poland, Russia took the field against Sweden, which was thought to have become weakened by the youth and inexperience of its teenage king Charles XII (1682–1718). But this war started out catastrophically for the anti-Swedish alliance: Denmark was quickly defeated and withdrew, while Poland, domestically divided as had become the norm, was hardly a factor. The Russians suffered a crushing defeat at Narva in 1700, which cost them almost all their artillery. In a desperate response, church bells were hauled down across the Russian empire to be recast as cannon.

The Swedes failed to press the advantage against Russia, however, mainly campaigning in Poland in subsequent years. This allowed Peter to recover, and even to order the building of St Petersburg on nominally Swedish territory in 1703. Poland surrendered to Sweden in 1706 and concluded a separate peace, after which Charles XII moved into Russian-ruled territory. After a long, drawn-out campaign, the Russians were victorious at Poltava in 1709. Charles, who fled to the Turks, did not give up yet, but, although the Great Northern War lasted until 1721, the Swedes were largely reduced to efforts to minimize their losses.

Peter might have ended the war after Poltava, but became overconfident. In 1711, allied with the Prince of Moldavia, the tsar moved into Ottoman territory, in part because he demanded that the Turks hand over Charles to him, in part because he underestimated the continued military strength of the Ottomans. He was severely beaten by the Turks at the Battle of the Pruth. Although wholly at the mercy of their grand vizir, Peter managed to extricate himself, even if it cost him Azov again. While the war with Sweden dragged on for another decade, without too many clear-cut victories for either side (the Poles and Danes rejoined the Russians after Poltava), it did witness Russia's – rather farcical – first victory in a sea battle, at Gangut near Finland in 1714. However minor this victory was (in this it was not unlike Kulikovo), it was to be cherished in Russian collective memory as one of the greatest battles ever won by the country.

Peter was awarded the title of *imperator* by his 'grateful Senate' upon the conclusion of the Peace of Nystadt with Sweden in 1721. The creation of this Senate (a body styled after that of Classical Rome) was one of the many domestic reforms Peter oversaw while waging war. By the mid-1710s, St Petersburg had replaced Moscow as the Russian capital during a frantic building boom that saw the city rise from a swamp. The *strel'tsy* disappeared after 1700, with the imperial guards taking their place, in a sense. *Boyar*s were given Western-European titles (*baron*, *graf*). Women, hitherto forced to live in seclusion, were suddenly permitted to show themselves in public. Dress changed, men's beards were shaved off, caftans were replaced by knickerbockers (*briuki*). The patriarch was replaced as head of the church by a lay official, the *Oberprokuror*. Plans were drawn up for a Russian Academy of Sciences, which opened just after Peter's death in 1725. Not only ships' wharves, but textile manufactories were founded, especially to sew uniforms for the army. Iron mining and arms manufacturing took flight.

In 1722 a Table of Ranks was introduced, which made it possible to gain noble status for commoners who received army commissions or joined the civil service. To some extent (as this only affected those who were not enserfed), merit replaced birth in distinguishing the various estates (*soslovye*) in Russia. The tsar's government ordained as well that all non-serfs had to serve the state, as did the tsar himself. It was far from a well-oiled machine, but in principle all were now engaged in furthering Russian greatness and glory. The 1721 Peace of Nystadt had not added much territory to Russia (mainly northern Latvia, Estonia, and St Petersburg and its environs), but when Peter died a few years later he had laid the groundwork of a much more viable empire. His successors proceeded to add ever more territory to the realm, steadily beating back all adversaries and moving Russia's borders further westward into Europe.

Peter's reforms were probably timely, since they allowed the Russian empire to survive another two hundred years. His sort of renovation seems to be part of the history of all long-lasting empires, so maybe some sort of constant can be recognized in such reformatory episodes regarding the lifespan of empires. The Roman Empire, after all, underwent wholesale political change in the days of Caesar and Augustus, and then again at the end of the third century, in response to significantly changed circumstances. The fall of the western part of the empire came in the fifth century, but even then its eastern part proved flexible enough to change again and survive as an empire until at least the Fourth Crusade. The Russian case seems not entirely dissimilar. The Muscovite Empire, which can be said to have started with Ivan III towards 1500, and survived an existential crisis just after 1600, was transformed into the Russian Empire by Peter the Great. Another two hundred years, and another wholesale transformation was undertaken. Despite profuse professions otherwise, the Soviet Union in some quintessential ways remained a Russian empire. Perhaps, then, the Russian Empire only fell in 1991, half a millennium after its original creation. Unless, of course, today's Russian Federation is comparable to the Byzantine Empire as the surviving viable half of an even larger empire, and has, still, a long life ahead of it.

9

The Waning of the Middle Ground: The Russian, French and British Empires, 1721–1853

From around 1700 onwards, borderlands began to disappear in northern Eurasia. The Razin Rebellion of 1670–71, in which Don Cossacks were ringleaders but were joined by various other ethnic groups living in the lower Volga region, had been a response to the growing encroachment of the central government on the freedom of the periphery. It was followed by further uprisings that saw a loose coalition of Cossacks, Nogai Tatars, Bashkirs and others living along the lower Volga and Don region challenge Moscow's rule: the largest were the Bulavin rebellion of 1707 and 1708 and the Pugachev rebellion from 1773 to 1775. In part, this was a protest against Russian attempts to impose serfdom and to limit the number of warriors who could formally register as Cossacks, but it was also a protest by those who more generally began to feel the weight of Russian rule come down on them.

The Middle Ground was waning, as it was in North America after 1700. In what seems in hindsight a relentless process (it was much more happenstance in reality), Russia began to colonize its borderlands at the easternmost extremity of Europe and in west Asia: Slavic settlers appeared and the number of government bureaucrats and soldiers increased.[1] The most remarkable response to this process was the 1771 exodus by the nomadic Kalmyks from their grasslands located in the steppe

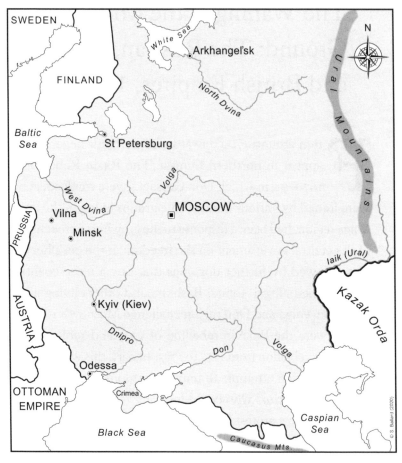

European Russia under Catherine the Great.

north of the Caspian Sea. They moved back to the region in Middle Asia from which in the early seventeenth century they had originally migrated westward. Such a radical step showed that resistance to increasing control by the central government might not yet seem wholly futile, even if the Kalmyks ended up submitting to the Chinese Qing Empire, which had been advancing westward.

From their outpost at Orenburg in Siberia, the Russians persuaded the trio of loosely organized states (*orda*s) of the Kazakhs to recognize Anna Ioannovna (r. 1730–40) as their sovereign. Initially, the Kazakhs mainly allied with the Russians because they needed support against the neighbouring Kalmyks and Bashkirs who harassed them, following the traditions of the *sherty*. Throughout much of the eighteenth and early nineteenth centuries, the Kazakh-Russian relationship remained one of partners rather than of lords and vassals. Only by the 1830s had the Russians gathered enough military strength, backed by sufficient funds, to truly impose their authority on the Kazakhs.

In many ways this ultimate Russian subjugation was the consequence of the ongoing military revolution, which towards 1800 began to make the tsar's armies vastly superior when fighting in open battles over irregular formations such as Cossack or Kazakh armies. While Bashkirs, Kazakhs or various Caucasian communities violently resisted for long periods, the Cossacks increasingly turned to bargaining in a rather successful effort to acquire a privileged position within the Imperial Russian state. Cossack chiefs were co-opted by the imperial government by giving them Russian noble titles and privileges. The rank-and-file Cossack warriors began to serve in the Russian military, as border guards, or, if necessary, as riot police. In the wake of the Pugachev rebellion, the Ukrainian Cossack hetmanate was abolished in 1775, their headquarters at Zaporizhiya destroyed. But while their independence was curtailed, the Cossacks of Ukraine, Russia and Siberia became in essence a privileged group or estate (*soslovye*).

Similar to Cossack hetmans, some of the leading Caucasian chiefs, such as those of the Cherkess or the Georgians, joined the Russian elite after they realized they could no longer beat back the tsar's military. Meanwhile, the Table of Ranks placated more restless or ambitious types among all of the tsar's peoples: codifying a tantalizing array of privileges and rewards for those who joined the tsarist team, it further bridled ethnic leaders' ambitions to challenge Russia's power.

It is significant that by Catherine II's time (that is, the second half of the eighteenth century) the Russian government began to make a distinction between Eastern Slavs and 'people of other origin', *inorodtsy*, among whom were Finno-Ugrians, Kazakhs, Tatars or Yakuts, who had previously fallen under the rubric of *inovertsy*, 'people of a different belief'. A mere recognition of religious difference began to make way for a more general sense of cultural superiority over 'uncivilized' people. By the time of the Crimean War (1853–6) a clear sense of Russian superiority is manifest in the government's policies *vis-à-vis* non-Russians. In this – ultimately racist – discourse, culture, religion and ethnicity all combined to make the Russians the empire's superior 'leading nation' (contemporary Germans used the untranslatable *Kulturträger* for such a group bearing an 'advanced civilization', tasked to rule those who had not seen the light). This Russian version of Rudyard Kipling's nineteenth-century 'white man's burden' mandated a civilizing mission to raise blighted fellow tsarist subjects up to lofty Russian levels of *kulturnost'* ('cultured behaviour'). As a consequence, Russification policies gathered force after 1850, and were even imposed on Ukrainians and Belarusians, who were considered backward Russians speaking a primitive rustic dialect.

Although the Soviet regime at first loudly denounced any distinctions among its subjects on the basis of ethnic groups' alleged advance towards human perfectibility, it seems Stalin, a Russian-acculturated Georgian, and his cronies could not wholly rid themselves of the idea that Russians somehow were a step ahead of the others. In 1945 Stalin unequivocally lauded the Russian people as the first among equals, the elder brother who set the example in the absurdly costly effort to defeat Hitler's Germany. He had in fact earlier, in the 1930s, signalled that the Russians were a cut above their fellow Soviets, which reflected how in the Soviet Union it was still Russian culture and language that primarily held sway. In the Soviet empire, Russian acculturation remained an advantage to get ahead in life. It is too much of a stretch to consider joining the ranks of the Communist Party as similar to entering the Table of Ranks, but, like the Table, Party membership offered an avenue to joining the imperial elite for Russians and non-Russians alike.

The tsars and tsarinas from Peter all the way to Nicholas I (r. 1825–55) behaved more and more as autocrats. The tacit power-sharing arrangement between *boyar*s and tsar had been shattered by Peter. But some descendants of the *boyar*s (such as the Dolgorukovs or Vorontsovs) maintained great influence at the court. At times of crisis, aristocrats of old stock and new stakeholders, upstarts who had risen during Peter's time and their descendants, or those who began to climb the ladder of the Table of Ranks, might join forces. If a tsar acted too indiscriminately against the interests of all these groups, he could come to grief at the hands of their coalition, as befell tsars Peter III in 1762 and Paul in 1801. These palace coups ensured that the mutually beneficial balance of power between tsar and ruling (albeit changing) elite was informally maintained, with both sides formally professing allegiance to an unrestrained tsarist autocracy as the empire's principle of government.

But the Enlightenment (c. 1730–90) and the French Revolution (1789–99) did begin to shake up the ideological foundations of the Russian empire, or, to be a bit more precise, caused the autocrat and others to justify much more consciously and publicly the legitimacy of their imperial authority. Catherine the Great (1729–1796), a native of the Holy Roman Empire, was influenced by her reading of a variety of Enlightenment texts, such as those by Cesare Beccaria (1738–1794), and eventually corresponded with Voltaire (1694–1778), while hosting Diderot (1713–1784) in St Petersburg. Even so, she staunchly defended her autocracy, which was hardly in the spirit of the Enlightenment. Under the influence of Beccaria's ideas, she did ponder the need for a more equitable, less arbitrary and savage jurisprudence than was customary in Russia, and made some changes in this regard. Nothing, however, was fundamentally accomplished in having Russia adopt a set of basic laws to which all were accountable, including the sovereign.

Catherine's greatest problem was that her legitimacy as empress was challenged by the hereditary law of succession. Her husband Peter III (1728–1762), as a descendant of one of Peter the Great's daughters, had succeeded his aunt Elisabeth (Elizaveta) in 1762, as he was the nearest blood relative of this empress. Prior to his accession, his right to rule was accepted even if by upbringing he was culturally a German, and religiously a Protestant. Quickly antagonizing everyone at court after succeeding, though, Peter had been first confined and then killed, with Catherine's knowledge, in 1762. As the male heir, Catherine's son Paul now might have been proclaimed tsar, with the eight-year-old boy being assisted by a regency council. Instead, Catherine excluded Paul from any say in government affairs until she died, 34 years later. She could justify her actions by referring to Peter the Great's decision to end primogeniture after he had disowned his oldest son and had him executed as a traitor, which left the throne subsequently open to the most capable member of the tsarist family upon the death of the reigning monarch.

Even if she was much better at pleasing various court factions and the Imperial Guards (whose officers had executed the coup) than her husband, her claims to the throne were dubious. She had no Romanov blood in her veins and traditional succession customs could always be resurrected as an excuse to overthrow her. She deemed it wiser, therefore, not to encourage too much discourse about the foundations of her rule as empress. As she somewhat flippantly wrote to Voltaire at some point, it was all nice and well to think and write about the most just and equitable principles of government, but he wrote on parchment whereas she had to write on human skin. In her view, it was for the moment best not to consider ambitious plans for a political overhaul in which power was shared between various branches of government, as had become the practice in the contemporary United Kingdom.

Implicitly, Catherine used a further argument not to tinker with unrestrained autocracy, which was the startlingly low educational level of almost all of her subjects. It seemed the height of irresponsibility to allow barely literate adults to have any say in the affairs of her empire. She treated her subjects as children, going as far as starting the first Russian periodicals in her country herself, as no one else was apparently schooled enough to do so. Once one of her subjects, Nikolai Novikov (1744–1818), started his own magazine, his efforts were fairly quickly shut down because they expressed a mildly critical voice.

Belying Catherine's argument that her subjects were uniformly illiterate bumpkins, many among the Russian elite in Catherine's day preferred to converse in French, the fashionable eighteenth-century language.[2] The Russians only fell out of love with this habit during the Napoleonic Wars around 1800. The 1812 invasion and the patriotic upsurge that followed the French withdrawal from Russia proved especially fatal to this French infatuation. One may question the actual proficiency in French of those who adopted it, but the highest circles employed French governesses, while, since Peter the Great's reign, children were often sent abroad, and parents travelled across the continent. Catherine II's rationale for treating her subjects as dimwits, then, did not quite add up.

This love affair with French culture and language originated perhaps in Peter the Great's sense of inferiority with regards to the Western Europeans, although he was rather more in awe of the English and Dutch than of the French. This inferiority complex became diffused among most of the Russian noble elite from Peter's reign onward. Once France became the leading paragon of European sophistication, Russian nobles adopted as much of French culture as possible. There were moments when a chauvinistic desire flared up throughout the eighteenth century against too much 'fawning before the West' (and there had been a reaction against the 'Germanized' court of Anna Ioannovna as well), but surges of Russian patriotism remained in their infancy before 1812. The first signs of the astonishing flourishing of Russian literature in the nineteenth century might be found before 1800, but today few outside Russia read the works composed by people such as Antiokh Kantemir (1708–1744), Aleksandr Sumarokov (1717–1777), or Denis Fonvizin (1744–1792). Mikhail Lomonosov (1711–1765), 'the first Russian scientist', studied and taught at Moscow University, but his myth is much greater than the man.[3] He was mainly a dilettante with a great imagination and probably should be considered as a less accomplished scientist than Iakov Brius (1669–1735), a scion of a Scottish mercenary family, a talented scientist and military engineer beloved by Peter the Great. A final culmination of this Russian inferiority complex can be found in Pyotr Chaadaev's (1794–1856) *Philosophical Letters*, which were distributed in unprinted form around 1830 (they did not pass censorship's muster). Chaadaev argued that Russian culture had never yielded anything worthwhile to offer humanity. While one might have pointed at Russian Orthodox iconography, for example, to counter Chaadaev's withering criticism, his thesis soon proved obsolete through the veritable cultural flourishing that was under way while he wrote his diatribe. Afterwards, the 1830s and '40s were dubbed the Golden Age of Russian culture. Its most outstanding exponent was the writer and poet Aleksandr Pushkin (1799–1837).

One key figure does herald the transition from an inchoate or inarticulate Russian imperial consciousness to a much more robust and unapologetic imperial identity: Nikolai Karamzin

(1766–1826).[4] A friend and defender of Novikov, Karamzin started out as an adherent of the Enlightenment before concluding that the implementation of its ideas might be disastrous, after he visited revolutionary France and saw the havoc when they were put into practice from 1789 onward. This Russian counterpart to Edmund Burke (1729–1797) then developed his own brand of conservatism, which upheld autocracy as the ideal kind of government for the tsar's empire. The tsar for whom Karamzin wrote, Alexander I (r. 1801–25), had been flirting in the early years of his reign with the idea of modernizing Russia following certain Enlightenment principles regarding human freedom and government accountability. As a child, his grandmother Catherine the Great had taken him away from the custody of his father, the later Paul I (r. 1796–1801), and had Alexander and his younger brother Constantine educated by the minor Swiss Enlightenment figure Frédéric César de La Harpe (1754–1838).

As we saw, Catherine had toyed with the idea that her grandsons might rule parallel empires one day, with Alexander ruling Russia from St Petersburg and Constantine from Constantinople (Istanbul), a reborn Orthodox Greek empire that would replace the destroyed Ottoman Empire. Catherine's plans for an all-out Christian offensive to dislodge the Turks, however, came apart once Austria became distracted by the French Revolution. Marie Antoinette (1755–1793), a sister of the Austrian emperor, was caught in the middle of the French turmoil and, rather than fighting the Turks, the Austrians entered a war with the French revolutionaries in 1792. When the Poles tried one last time to restore full independence from the Russian, Austrian and Prussian patronage they had been forced to endure since the 1770s, the complicated diplomatic and military manoeuvres towards a second, in 1793, and third and definitive, in 1795, Polish partition further shelved any ideas of a comprehensive victory over the Turks.

Catherine had imagined her grandsons' empires as havens of enlightened European civilization, but what that exactly meant remained unclear, as she had done little to introduce any kind of enlightened civilization during her reign in Russia. And as unclear as Catherine was on the implementation of Enlightenment ideas in practice, as hesitant was her grandson Alexander I about introducing meaningful reforms when he took the reins after the murder of his father (which he had condoned). Alexander established an advisory council made up of likeminded friends, but his reformatory policies were cautious and limited in scope. He abolished serfdom in the Baltic region, but the emancipated peasants there received no lands. This merely transformed them into landless people, forced to hire themselves out as agricultural labourers to their former landlords. He founded a few more universities, but any further truly meaningful progressive reforms never went beyond the planning stage.

Like his grandmother, Alexander I was to acquire the greatest renown instead for his successful foreign policy and military victories, making Russia into the hegemon of the European continent. The first clashes between Russia and Napoleonic France went the French way, but the battles of Austerlitz (1805) and Friedland (1807), fought beyond Russia's borders, were far from decisive French triumphs. The Treaty of Tilsit between Alexander and Napoléon I (1769–1821) of 1807 allowed the Russians to firm up their claims in the Caucasus. Already in 1783 Georgia had submitted to Russia to stave off an Ottoman threat, a submission that formally became a Russian annexation in 1801. The Turks and Russians tried to expand their dominion over the Caucasus region in the face of a floundering Iran, the traditional overlord of a large part of this mountainous region. In 1804 Russians and Iranians were engaged in an open war, which lasted until 1813. The Treaty of Gulistan with which the conflict ended had Iran recognize Russian hegemony not only over Georgia, but over Dagestan, a large stretch of territory along the Caspian Sea, and northern Azerbaijan. Part of the northwestern Caucasus continued to pay homage to the sultan in Istanbul, but the Turks were hardly in a position after 1800 to come to the rescue of the various small Muslim populations who resided there, such as the Cherkessians, Chechens or Ingushetians.[5]

Thus, while fending off Napoléon, Russia was extending its hold southward, capitalizing on the declining strength of the Ottomans and Iranians. Russian Europe, though, briefly faced an existential crisis not unlike that of the 1610s, which might have made Russia into a secondary power. Certainly, Napoléon may have fallen victim to hubris, and one is left to wonder what would have happened if he had concentrated on halting the burgeoning rebellion in Spain after 1810 and avoided any campaigning into Russian territory. Still, the 600,000 men who crossed the border from the French satellite state that was the Grand Duchy of Warsaw into Russia made more meaningful territorial progress than Hitler's military in 1941, occupying Moscow in 1812. But Napoléon was not sure how to proceed once Moscow was captured, ultimately ordering a withdrawal at a disastrous moment. Somehow he felt that his army, which had lost large numbers of troops in the long march across Russia, was better off moving back towards Poland during the worst of autumn's muddy season (*rasputitsa*), which was followed by the frost of winter.

Scholarship has insufficiently explained why the French emperor deemed it best to send his main army to Moscow (a minor force was sent into Lithuania) rather than St Petersburg, the Russian capital, where the tsar resided.[6] Despite Moscow's fall, then, the war of 1812 turned into a catastrophe for the French and probably the greatest Russian-imperial military victory, even if besides at Borodino no major battles were fought. The Russian army further pursued this stunning victory by joining the 'Battle of the Nations' at Leipzig in 1813 and entering Paris in 1814. At the Congress of Vienna in 1814 and 1815, Alexander I was the most powerful monarch present, for his only rival, the British king, was absent, and merely represented by his foreign minister Castlereagh (1769–1822). But an opportunity was missed at Vienna to lay down a truly durable or stable settlement that could guarantee Europe's and Russia's peace in the long term.

By 1814 Alexander had turned against the Enlightenment ideals of his youth, becoming a sort of mystically inclined traditionalist Christian more interested in spiritual matters than in establishing a workable protocol for international peace in this world. Only very myopic observers can maintain that Vienna laid the groundwork for a century of European or global peace.[7] In a number of crises after 1815 – such as those over Greece and Belgium, and, after 1840, the Opium Wars, the Crimean War, the Russo-Turkish War, the Russo-Japanese War, the Spanish-American War, or the Balkan Wars – various European powers clashed directly, or through proxies, long before 1914. If Alexander could have found a more solid understanding with France and Britain in particular, some of these conflicts might have been avoided. What was worse for Russia, perhaps, was that, after the Greek War of Independence of the 1820s, Russia usually drew the short end of the stick, or was ignored, in all these conflicts. Alexander, in other words, too easily spent Russia's credit at Vienna.

The year 1812 seems to have been the crucial moment in changing Alexander's worldview. We are not sure as to how far Karamzin's 1812 memorandum mentioned earlier was the trigger, or how far Alexander had already determined that any fundamental change was hazardous for Russia's survival, but he did abandon any plans for significant reform after the French onslaught on his country. Thereafter he listened to a number of religious zealots and even spiritualists such as Madame de Krüdener (1764–1824). Religious universalism, rather than secular peace and justice, and esotericism now occupied the tsar's mind. (Many have made the link with an unbearable sense of guilt plaguing him about the violent death of his father.) Not yet fifty years old, Alexander died in 1825 during a sojourn at Taganrog in the south of his country.[8]

Imperial Russia possibly reached its apex as an empire in 1815. In that year, the Russian empire may have reached a saturation point, after which it fell victim to what Paul Kennedy called 'imperial overstretch'.[9] The Russian shoreline along the Baltic Sea stretched from southern Lithuania's coast to that of northern Finland; even Alaska, the coastal areas of what are now the Yukon and British Columbia provinces of Canada, and of what are today's Washington and Oregon states, were nominally under Russian rule; Russia ruled Siberia; both the Caucasus and what is now Kazakhstan were part of its sphere of influence; and the tsar ruled by far the greatest part of the former Rzeczpospolita. It had few competitors globally. The only true rival after the Napoleonic Wars seemed to be the British Empire, but before 1850 it was very reticent about being an empire, haunted by the loss of the Thirteen Colonies. Indeed, the entire British imperial project possibly hung in abeyance. In hindsight, this proved to be more of a transition phase for the United Kingdom than any step towards abandonment of its imperial ambitions, but for several decades after 1815 Britain *seemed* more interested in controlling trading or supply ports for its long-distance shipping than in expanding, or even exercising, territorial control. The simultaneously raging First Afghan War and First Opium War (both 1839–42) seemed to confirm that British interest was more than anything else in trade. The first of these wars aimed at territorial control and ended in defeat, the second aimed at the expansion of trade and ended in victory. It was during the First Afghan War, meanwhile, that Britain became more aware of a potential clash with Russia, which had cautiously begun its advance deeper into Middle Asia.

Otherwise, after 1815 a number of once glorious empires were on life support. Spain was in the process of surrendering its continental American empire; the Austrian Habsburgs were reeling from their slew of crushing defeats at the hands of Napoléon (who had even married a Habsburg princess to add insult to injury); Prussia would not recover before 1860; France was licking its wounds. The Ottoman Turks were quickly becoming the 'sick man of Europe', more and more propped up by other powers, while the extreme isolation of China and Japan became gradually unsustainable in a world in which technological change had suddenly through the advent of industrialization taken on far greater significance. For more than a century, the Moghul emperor's power in India had drastically eroded, and it was mainly British reluctance to provide a deathblow that kept it alive for another few decades. In comparison, Russia seemed vigorous and healthy, ready to fill in whichever power vacuum might arise across Eurasia.

But it was its very success that bred complacency. Before the 1840s, Russia (that is, its court and broader government circles) seems to have completely ignored that other revolution that began to unfold after 1780, the Industrial Revolution. Of course, others, too, woke up slowly to the breathtaking changes overtaking the United Kingdom. On the European continent by the time Belgium began to industrialize thirty to forty years had passed since England and Scotland had entered the process; France followed Belgium, but it began to industrialize only very slowly after 1820, with modern factories and mines that used mechanized production processes appearing in just a few regions. The German lands only turned wholeheartedly to industrialization after 1840, as did the northeastern USA.

And thus Russia's economy proved stunningly backward in the Crimean War. Called on to fight the British, French, Turkish and Sardinian armies, Russia was severely handicapped in this conflict by its lack of railways and modern ships, as well as its technologically backward weaponry. In the preceding years, Russia had not been wholly blind to the novelties of the new age: the first railway had opened under Tsar Nicholas I (r. 1825–55), but this had not stirred up any Russian entrepreneurial spirit. Russia remained truly two generations behind Britain in terms of technological development, while the effort to catch up only really picked up speed even much later, in the 1870s. The gap with the most advanced industrialized countries was never sufficiently made up before 1914, which was all the more catastrophic because Russia was so much larger in territorial size than its competitors. Much more rail track than in Germany or Austria-Hungary needed to be laid to transport Russia's military and its hardware, for the Russian borders were so much longer and its hinterland so much larger.

At the point that Nicholas I succeeded his brother in December 1825, he immediately became the first tsar to be challenged by an opposition that called for major political reform. The Decembrists, many of whom were officers in the Imperial Guards, demanded a constitution, as had become the norm in Europe and elsewhere after the American and French Revolutions. But the Decembrists lacked much backing, and both those who attempted to lead a coup in St Petersburg and their allies in Kyiv and elsewhere were easily apprehended by the tsarist authorities. Five of the ringleaders were sentenced to death and executed, while many more received lifelong sentences of Siberian exile. Their protest seemed to fall on deaf ears in most of Russian society, which remained timid and highly reluctant to challenge the divinely ordained autocrat.

Nicholas I resembled his grandmother Catherine the Great in believing that his subjects were incapable of thinking for themselves. They needed to be ruled by his firm hand: only he was able to censor such a genius as Pushkin. Still, Nicholas concluded that his empire needed some sort of positive response to the French Revolution and its slogans about liberty, equality and universal brotherhood. He therefore backed his education minister Sergei Uvarov (1786–1855), when the latter suggested a more self-conscious imperial ideology based on the three principles of autocracy, nationality and orthodoxy.

The first element of this ideology meant a continued adherence to the principle of one-man rule, with a succession that was based on primogeniture, as it had been since Paul's reign. (It should be remembered that the principle of the oldest son succeeding had been previously abolished by Peter the Great.)

No plans were entertained to have the tsar account for his actions to any public forum or legislature. Nationality meant a general support for a generic Russian (*rossiiskii*) identity that rejected foreign contamination. It remained unclear how non-Slavs in particular were to fit into this concept, but if the population of Poles, Ukrainians, Belarusians and Russians (*russkie*) in the empire were counted as *rossiiskii*, that is as Russian-imperial, it could be said that the empire counted only a fairly small minority of non-Slavs or non-*rossiiskii* people. Obviously, the question was the extent to which Poles, Ukrainians or Belarusians were truly willing to consider an ethnic Russian tsar as their 'own' sovereign. Few among the politically articulate Polish elite were willing to accept the emperor as the legitimate successor of the king of Poland-Lithuania. Neither was the tsar the true ruler for many educated Ukrainians, even if such opponents constituted a much smaller proportion of the Ukrainian population than the proportion of Poles who rejected Russian rule. Ukrainian intellectuals rejected both the tsar's claim to be either the descendant of the Kyivan rulers or of the Zaporizhiyan *atamany*. Nonetheless, Nicholas could argue that such objections were only raised by a small minority of noble or intellectual Poles and Ukrainians, and that the great majority of largely illiterate people in the western parts of his empire might easily be persuaded to be loyal to the tsar.

Adherence to Orthodoxy was far from universal in Nicholas's empire, and perhaps Uvarov's programme was least persuasive in this respect. Indeed, in 1820 the tsar's older brother Konstantin had married a Catholic Polish noblewoman, Joanna Grudzinska (1795–1831), who never converted to Orthodoxy.[10] Concerted efforts to convert the tsar's non-Orthodox subjects to Greek Christianity had never been undertaken in any consistent fashion, and Nicholas did not change much in this respect. In an age when religion still trumped other identity markers, any mass proselytizing was a hazardous undertaking. On two occasions, though, the tsar acted as a true champion of Orthodoxy in his *foreign* policy. In the first case, the outcome was a success: Greece became independent from the Ottoman Empire in 1830, not least thanks to the feats of the Russian navy. But in the second case, the tsar overplayed his hand against the Turks, and was confronted with France and Britain as opponents in the Crimean War, rather than his allies as they had been in the Greek war.

Regardless, at home autocracy, nationality and orthodoxy remained a limp, lifeless concept, which gained little traction. At most it meant a refurbished adherence to traditional supranational ideas of political loyalty to the 'tsar-little father' and to Orthodox-Christian tradition. Intended as a more modern imperialist ideology, it never quite succeeded.

10

Indirect and Direct Rule: The Russian and British Empires in Asia, 1853–1907

The defeat in the Crimean War led Nicholas I's successor, Alexander II, to seek another strategy to generate a more deeply felt and widespread enthusiasm among his peoples for the Russian empire than the unappealing ideological triad his father had propagated. This had an immediate and urgent purpose, as the poor military performance in the war was linked to the poor morale of the soldiers. It was believed that the troops had fought listlessly because they had little to fight for, as many were serfs who lacked rights and possessions. 'Empire' to them was an abstract and meaningless concept that had very little to do with their daily lives: they hardly felt part of this entity.

In addition, Russia was the only country in Europe that still preserved serfdom when Alexander II succeeded in 1855. It was seen as an obsolete institution and provided evidence for those at home and abroad who called the Russian empire backward, an odious word in an age of ceaseless economic and technological progress. Alexander II and his advisors decided to implement significant reforms to precipitate popular enthusiasm and support for the Russian empire and have it catch up with Britain and France, the paragons of progress. Serfdom was abolished in much of European Russia in 1861, with most former serfs given a piece of land upon their release from bondage, although their former lords kept significant amounts of it. As noted in the first chapter, the terms of the serfs' emancipation from their lords were differentiated, and this lack of uniformity led to complaints and protests that lessened the initial enthusiasm for the tsar's magnanimous decree. Compensation payments to the former lords, to be paid into a state bank, further dampened the spirit. Subsequent reforms introduced a measure of self-government and the principle of equality before the law, but were again calibrated regionally, privileging some territories over others, while such changes did not uniformly apply to all estates. And the introduction of military conscription in 1874 excluded numerous non-Russian regions. Even when it constituted in European Russia a vast improvement for the male population, because it reduced the years of active service for illiterate recruits from 25 to six years, and for those with some education even further, it added to the sense of inequitable treatment felt by some: once again, select groups were given preferential treatment because of ethnicity or estate. All of these perceived injustices hurt Alexander II's attempt to increase the popular support for his empire, a motive that in some measure had spurred him on to undertake his reform programme. Rather than the profound gratitude of his subjects, he was met with criticism, while his policies to reduce his father's close monitoring of his people again allowed revolutionary groups to organize. In 1866, a first attempt on his life was undertaken; in 1881 he was assassinated.

Although industrialization (its beginnings can be traced to Alexander II's rule) came late to Russia when compared to Western countries, the empire's military was markedly advanced in technological terms if compared to most Asian armies after 1800. While Russian artillery and hand-held firearms were

Russian 19th-century expansion into Central Asia.

superior to those of their enemies, it was more important that Russia's armies were backed by the taxation revenue regularly collected from tens of millions of people. It sustained the armies in the field against the forces of much smaller polities, whether in the Caucasus or Central Asia. The Crimean War was a disaster for Russia, but this was not because of the strength of the Ottoman-Turkish military. Facing Turkey in isolation, Russia was stronger, as it proved to be in the war of 1877 and 1878. The Turkish government was not as adept at collecting the funds needed to fight a modern war. By 1858, China, facing French and British forces along its southern coasts, was powerless to stop Russia from abrogating the terms of the 1689 Treaty of Nerchinsk. The borders with Qing China in eastern Siberia were considerably moved southward. The port of Vladivostok was founded with the aim of significantly increasing the Russian role in East Asia.

After this, the Russian influence in Mongolia and Manchuria markedly grew. The tottering Chinese empire could no longer put up any meaningful resistance, beset by British, French, Japanese, Germans and Russians all at the same time. The somewhat pathetic Boxer Rebellion of 1900, which saw Chinese martial arts' experts trying to fight Russian-manned machine guns with fists, swords and nunchucks, brutally underlined China's obsolescence. In Manchuria and Korea, however, the Russians increasingly clashed with the far more formidable, modernizing Japanese. Woken up to a new age by the arrival of an American naval squadron at Tokyo Bay in the 1850s, the Japanese tried to increase their influence in East Asia. As a result of this rude awakening, Japan began to industrialize at about the same time as Russia, and it proved much more adept.

Building the railway to Murmansk across the Kola peninsula, 1915.

In 1894 war broke out between Japan and China over Korea. Within a year the Chinese were defeated, but the Russians, who had been interested bystanders, were unwilling to allow Japan to enjoy all the spoils of its victory. Grudgingly, Japan struck a deal with Russia. Between each other, the two countries divided control over Manchuria and Korea. The Russian government, however, failed to understand how important the role of the Western powers was in propping up this agreement; and whereas France and Germany were willing to placate the Russians in the Far Eastern theatre, Britain was much more reluctant to do so, as it saw Russia's moves in this region as part of the unfolding of a comprehensive Russian strategy across Asia that threatened British interests.

This 'Great Game', a sort of cold war between Russia and Britain that lasted for more than half a century, from the 1850s to the early 1900s, was an imperialist chess game across much of Asia eastward of the Caucasus. It never led to open war between the two rivals (after 1856, at least), but both sides feared each other in their efforts, by way of a game of manoeuvre and counter-manoeuvre, to take over the remnants of the Iranian, Mughal and Qing empires, as well as to subjugate the various polities ruling Turkestan and Afghanistan. The Great Game concluded in 1907 with a qualified British victory.

It was as much as anything the outcome of the Japanese-Russian conflict that decided the British-Russian rivalry to British advantage. The Japanese, backed by the British, comprehensively defeated the Russians in a war in 1904 and 1905. It began when Russia was surprised by a Japanese attack on Port Arthur, a Manchurian harbour Russia leased from the Chinese government. None of the European powers came to its defence; subsequently, Russia was humiliated by the Japanese navy in the Tsushima Straits and by its army at Mukden in 1905. These defeats at the hands of an Asian country triggered a revolutionary situation in European Russia that almost ended the Romanov dynasty.

By the early 1900s, theoretical racism had become the norm, as we saw from the manner in which the Russians justified their hegemony within the tsar's empire: Europeans felt racially superior to Asians. The Japanese victory was a powerful blow to the Russian self-image, and to its reputation as a powerful empire in the world, since most Russians wanted to be considered wholly European; subsequently, Russia desperately tried to recover from this loss of face. The desire to regain some of its lost prestige in the Russo-Japanese War informed the decision not to de-escalate the crisis of 1914.

Before the Russo-Japanese War halted any further expansionist ambitions, the Russian empire had expanded significantly in the second half of the nineteenth century, not just in East Asia. In the northwestern Caucasus, Russian rule was not established before a decades-long struggle had been fought against tenacious local rulers backed by the zealous support of several small Muslim ethnic communities. The difficult conditions of the terrain hindered the Russian military's campaigns in this mountainous region. They showed how even superior weaponry and comparatively ample means do not always translate into an easy military victory. Only in the early 1860s did the

Dagestan before the 1917 revolution.

Imam Shamil (1797–1871) surrender, concluding thirty years of stubborn resistance to the imposition of Russian rule. Many of his followers refused to accept being governed by a Christian and left for the Ottoman Empire. At the cost of much bloodshed, Russia's occupation of the Caucasus was complete.

The story in Central Asia was different, but the causes of the defeat of the Kazakhs, Turkmen, Uzbeks and Kirghiz were similar: the Russians far outstripped their opponents in terms of the sophistication of their weaponry and the means with which they could sustain their operations. The Kazakhs had intermittently acknowledged the tsars since the eighteenth century, as we saw, but were gradually brought under firmer control by military campaigns originating in the string of

Hairdressers in Samarkand, 1910s.

Indirect and Direct Rule

Russian Imperial translator in the Eurasian steppe, *c*. 1910.

Siberian fortress-cities along the border of Siberia and northern Kazakhstan, and the foundation of new fortresses north of the Aral Sea.

The numerically small nomadic communities who made up the Kazakhs, as well as the Kirghiz who lived in regions further east nearer the Chinese borders, were no match for the Russian armies that faced them. There was some resistance, but most of the Kazakhs and Kirghiz recognized that it was better to join Russia than try to beat it.

Armed resistance was stronger in regions further south, where the Turkmen, Uzbeks and Tajiks resided. For logistical reasons, it was more difficult for the Russians in the 1860s, 1870s and 1880s to subjugate the emirates and khanates that

Isfandiar, Khan of Khorezm in Central Asia, *c.* 1910.

existed there. The distance that the Russian troops had to cover from their home base in Siberia was considerably longer, and at times their opponents could ensconce themselves in walled cities. Ultimately, the dogged Russian commanders made their technological superiority count, using brutal means if deemed useful. After the Russian capture of Geok Tepe in Turkmenistan in 1881, thousands of civilians were thus butchered.

This, the age of modern imperialism, saw Russia acquiring its Caucasian and Middle Asian territories when Great Britain laid claim to all of India and parts of Africa, and France subjugated Indochina and other parts of Africa. Colonization was justified by arguments that Europeans were obliged to bring inferior peoples to the light of civilization and modernity. Of course, as J. A. Hobson (1858–1940) suggested in the 1900s, much of the motivation of the British and French was in fact economic, the consequence of a search for new markets and resources for the booming industries of Europe.[1] A global economic depression began in 1873, which led European countries to increase import tariffs on foreign commodities to protect domestic manufacturing and agriculture, but this usually led to similar countermoves by rivalling European powers. Empire seemed to offer a solution: Britain had previously found a vast market for its textiles in India, for example, while palm oil, gold and diamonds were imported from its African colonies.

The Russian government thought to see potential in the cotton that could be grown in Central Asia. The textile mills of Poland and central Russia were among the empire's first modern factories. Working on behalf of the Russians, the Swedish brothers Nobel began to extract oil both near Azeri Baku and on the eastern shores of the Caspian Sea. Oil was not as much of a crucial resource in the 1880s as it is today, but its promise was evident. Still, much of Russia's economic potential remained undeveloped or underdeveloped before 1900. Its colonial adventure in Asia proved expensive rather than lucrative. Railways were laid, canals built, hospitals and schools founded, while a military and administrative apparatus had to be maintained; yet, little economic benefit ensued.

In Russia, too, colonial rule was justified by drawing on theories about racially based human inequality, which called upon Russians to take Asians by the hand and lead them to a better life. Of course, such theories also justified treating them brutally if they resisted Russian patronage. The Russian foreign minister Aleksandr Gorchakov (1798–1883) declared just after 1860 that, like other leading European powers, Russia had its own civilizing mission. This implied that it would bring such supposed blessings as railways, healthcare or schools to the alleged savages mired in ignorance that it had ruled for a while already, as in Siberia, or was in the process of subjugating, as in the Caucasus and Central Asia. The empire in its late nineteenth-century guise expressed the administrative elite's desire to have Russians considered one of the culture-bearing peoples of the world, called upon to carry their share of the white man's burden.

In fact, however, this attitude reflected a great degree of uncertainty: the Western powers as well as Germany, and to some extent Habsburg Austria-Hungary, doubted Russia's status as a *Kulturträger*, often deriding it as an 'oriental despotism', a barbaric Asian empire that belonged to the ranks of the Ottoman or Chinese empires. Even Karl Marx suggested this.[2] This made the Russian sense of humiliation felt after the defeat by the Japanese even more profound.

Despite their blustering, the Russians were, meanwhile, often reluctant 'civilizers' in practice: depending on the region, they moved from wholesale Russification of non-Russian territory in Russian Europe to a far more benevolent regime in which the non-Russians in Asia were allowed a fair amount of autonomy. Here, too, the dichotomy between '*russkii*' (Russian-nationalist, exclusivist) and '*rossiiskii*' (all-Russian, inclusive) becomes apparent.

In some regions, Russian-nationalist policies provoked a growing resistance among non-Russians. For example, by 1900 such measures as the gradual spread of Russian-language education as a part of an overall more sustained effort at increasing literacy amounted to a profound change in some people's lives in various non-Russian regions. In the Caucasus and Central Asia, though, the traditional policies of the Muscovite composite empire continued to be honoured. If schools were established, they offered education in the local language rather than Russian.[3] As long as local community leaders obeyed Russian administrators, paid their taxes and kept the peace among their flock, the Russians usually left the local culture alone in these parts. Some influence of modern Western or Russian ideas can be discerned in the spread of the modernist Islamic reform movement of Jadidism, counterparts of which could be found in contemporary Muslim societies outside Russia as well. Of course, modernity did attract some people in almost all of the non-Russian communities: for those keen to make a career in the Russian military and government,

Clerk in Bukhara, Central Asia, 1910s.

acculturation was an option, with the Table of Ranks offering a way into the civil service or military, and economic modernization attracting some entrepreneurial types. In this regard, the history of Russia's imperialism does differ from that of Britain or France.

The long-standing, indeed Muscovite, custom of co-opting non-Russian elites into the ruling stratum of the empire, and the non-discriminatory possibilities the Table of Ranks offered, may have increased the sustainability of the Russian empire, and provides something of a clue as to why the Soviets could resurrect their own version of it. In Britain, virtually no colonial subject entered its economic, military, political or social elite before 1945. The French and British had African or Asian

Mosque in Vladikavkaz, northern Caucasus, 1910s.

soldiers fight in their armies, but none of their higher officers were African or Asian. This was different in Russia. Georgians served as army commanders, Armenians were government ministers, and Polish and (largely German-speaking) Baltic nobles were numerous.

11
Multinational Empires: Russia and Austria-Hungary, 1853–1917

The most comprehensive census in the Russian empire was held in December 1896 and January 1897, counting slightly more than 125 million inhabitants.[1] It enumerated a bewilderingly large number of ethnocultural communities and languages over which Tsar Nicholas II (r. 1894–1917) held the sceptre. Nicholas's empire, too, started to show the impact of industrialization, as evidenced by the growing number of large urban settlements. People began to leave the relative isolation of their ancestral communities and migrate to the cities. The empire, though, was still more than anything populated by people living in rural dwellings. Barely more than 10 per cent of the population lived in towns.

Although in size covering less than a quarter of the empire, four-fifths of the tsar's subjects lived in European Russia (that is, today's Russia, Baltic countries, Finland, Ukraine, Belarus, Moldova and parts of Poland). The Caucasus and Transcaucasian region had about 10 million inhabitants. Siberia, encompassing more than half of the empire's territory, was home to fewer than 6 million people: its population density was less than one person per square kilometre. Slightly fewer than 8 million people lived in Russian-ruled Central Asia.

More than 55 million people indicated that Russian was their mother tongue, and more than 22 million were identified

Multinational Empires

as speaking *malorusskii* (Little Russian), that is, Ukrainian. The Ukrainian language, though, was not recognized by the census enumerators as a distinct language. Slightly fewer than 6 million spoke *belorusskii* (White Russian), again seen as a dialect rather than a language. Superficially, this will have given the tsar's court and the higher administrators comfort, for in their reading two-thirds of the imperial population was 'Russian' (*russkii*)-speaking. Seen in this light, the imperial-national project on which Tsar Alexander III (r. 1881–94) and his advisors had embarked in the previous decade made sense. Given the great preponderance of Russians they believed to see among their subjects, their policy of Russification seemed a promising avenue towards strengthening 'nationalist' loyalty to the tsar. Before 1905, Nicholas II saw indeed no reason to change his father's policy.

The last two tsars were undoubtedly inspired by similar projects that privileged one language in administration and education in other European countries such as France and Germany. And perhaps it could have worked. France in the 1880s was a country in which large minorities did not speak the *langue d'oïl* of the Ile de France, the centre of the country. Education minister Jules Ferry and other leading ministers feverishly worked at Frenchifying their population, making *French* men and women out of Bretons, Flemings, Basques, Catalans, Savoyards or people from the Languedoc. Their version of French became the common language of communication between all French citizens within a generation, in significant part thanks to compulsory primary education. Chancellor Otto von Bismarck (1815–1898) oversaw similar Germanizing policies in the newly created German empire, which enforced the use of *Hochdeutsch* over the various regional dialects, as well as over the Polish spoken by a number of people in formerly Polish-ruled areas.

But the last two emperors and their entourage failed to perceive that the Russian case was fundamentally different from that of France or Germany. Russia was far more like Austria-Hungary, a multinational empire (*Vielvölkerreich*) where no ethnocultural community formed a clear majority of the population. Any policy to favour one language and culture over others might provoke social and cultural leaders of those other 'nations' to assert their and their compatriots' identity in response. As Miroslav Hroch and others have pointed out, this could constitute the first stage of a process leading to the formation of a more pronounced national identity.[2] In the tsar's realm, such an adverse reaction to Russification initially often affected only a small minority of intellectuals and some of the leading social strata. But some of the non-Russians did resist the efforts to Russify in more substantial numbers. The 8 million Poles of the Russian empire were foremost among them.

Polish resistance to Russian rule was of course longstanding, and was rooted to some extent in the era before the eighteenth-century Partitions of Poland. The last of these had been executed in 1795 in response to a Polish nationalist revolt. This third partition had definitively wiped Poland off the map, but the Poles (meaning at first mainly some of its educated nobility) had never resigned themselves to this outcome. In the early 1800s, Poles had prevailed on Napoléon I to restore a quasi-independent Polish state, the Grand Duchy of Warsaw. Alexander I at Vienna decided that Polish nationalist sentiment was so strong that he needed to preserve formal Polish independence, even if he ruled Poland in a personal union: he was tsar in Russia and king in Poland at the same time.

Dissatisfied with the degree of independence they enjoyed, the Poles rose against Russian rule in 1830 and 1863, in both cases seeing the limited independence they previously enjoyed being further reduced, after each rebellion was suppressed by brute force. Tsar Alexander III seemed to aim at ending Polish identity altogether. Fearing even greater Russian brutality and oppression, Polish nationalists treaded carefully around 1900, but their desire for independence remained strong. By then, Polish nationalism had become something of a mass phenomenon; most Poles had been taught about their language and culture through an elaborate network of national educational institutions that had been organized outside of Russian state control, while the Polish Catholic Church also functioned as an instrument to galvanize a sense of Polishness.

The Poles did face the complication of having millions of their compatriots living in Germany and Austria. Others resided in Russian-ruled rural areas in which they were surrounded by a majority of Ukrainians or Belarusians. And although Catholic Poles lived in great number in the industrializing cities of the western stretches of the Russian empire, the towns of historical Poland were also populated by Russian bureaucrats and military, as well as Jews, whose mother tongue was Yiddish, and German-speakers who were often Lutheran. The Polish nationalist cause was therefore not clear-cut, and ethnic tensions therefore lingered in the independent Poland that re-emerged on the map of Europe in 1918. The complicated ethnocultural situation in Poland may explain why many of those living in the Polish regions of Russia tried to look beyond nationalism and joined the supranational revolutionary movements. Social Democrats and even the more rurally oriented Socialist Revolutionaries[3] had a large Jewish membership in territorially Polish areas. Even Catholic Poles such as Feliks Dzerzhinskii (1877–1926) joined the Russian left-wing opposition.

Perhaps guided by their tutor Konstantin Pobedonostsev's (1827–1907) unapologetic defence of their autocratic power, Alexander III and Nicholas II did not understand very well that their empire's historical expansion had often been the result of carefully calibrated agreements with a variety of ethnocultural minorities made by their predecessors. Those communities had been only very slowly integrated into their realm, and remained jealous of their autonomy. Cossacks, Kazakhs and Tatars had enjoyed an almost semi-independent status for decades, or even centuries; when they were brought under firmer control, this was done cautiously, so as not to offend ethnic and cultural sensibilities. Before 1881 Russian authorities usually proceeded with great caution and circumspection in the Caucasus and Transcaucasian regions, and in Central Asia as well as in Poland. In the Muslim areas they had done this more than elsewhere, in part because they did not want to challenge Islam, which often remained a much stronger identity marker for the Islamic population of the empire than any ethnic(-linguistic) allegiance. In contrast, in Finland and the Baltic region tolerance had given way to Russification policies, in the expectation that this should not cause much protest. This was a miscalculation, for Russification there gave rise to nationalist movements that within a generation became strong enough to guide their countries to independence.

But even when they soft-pedalled Russification in the non-Russian areas, the Russian resolute top-down method of government triggered growing resentment and opposition. Around 1900, nationalist movements gathered strength at the same time as socialist movements did, both united in their

Samarkand around 1900.

rejection of unrestricted tsarist autocracy. With perhaps the exception of Poland, the tsars might have been able to channel nationalist sentiment and deflect it from becoming anti-tsarist. The last Romanovs, however, were ham-fisted and lacked the political subtlety needed to take the sting out of nationalism. Rather than developing a sensible ethnocultural policy in dialogue with representatives from various non-Russian ethnic communities, they flirted instead with ultra-nationalist Russian movements such as the Union of the Russian People (the Black Hundreds), contributing to the further growth and radicalization of nationalism among the non-Russians.

Many twentieth-century historians have speculated that introducing a political system in which stakeholders could hold the government accountable for its actions might have broadened the support-base of the Romanovs. This might have saved the last tsar from affiliating with such fringe groups as the Black Hundreds and saved his crown. Still, while responsible government had been introduced in Austria-Hungary and Bismarckian Germany, it did not save either the Habsburg or the Hohenzollern dynasty in 1918. And Russia itself was no longer a true autocracy after October 1905. A case can be made that it was not that much different anymore from its western neighbours in terms of the principles of its political organization. Membership of the imperial Duma (parliament), however, did not cement a loyalty to the Romanov dynasty among the tsar's subjects and their political representatives strong enough to help it survive the desperate crisis into which the First World War threw Russia.

Nevertheless, before the First World War most ethnocultural communities (or perhaps more than anything their elites) continued to display a pride in being part of a *rossiiskii* empire, Poland being the one clear exception. Loyalty to the tsar, traditional deference to nobles and clergy, a strong degree of cultural autonomy in a number of regions, gradually increasing possibilities for economic betterment, lack of any meaningful alternative state, and weakly developed nationalism probably all explain this fairly widespread imperial(-ist) mindset. The responses to the census of 1896–7 indicate how religion usually trumped nationality in people's loyalties. Would the development of a democratic empire of equal nations, as the later Soviet pretense would have it, have been possible under the Romanovs?

A solution in a somewhat coherent fashion in this direction was first suggested for the Habsburg monarchy by the social

Multinational Empires

democrats Otto Bauer (1881–1938) and Karl Renner (1870–1950) in 1907.[4] A certain Russian revolutionary using the pseudonym K. Stalin responded in 1913 to their ideas with his one claim to early fame as a theoretician: *Marxism and the Nationality Question*.[5] Stalin suggested here a sort of administrative dividing up of the Russian empire into federally affiliated large regions, such as Ukraine, or the Caucasus. In this sort of voluntary confederacy, the rights of minorities, such as for example Jews or Russians in Ukraine, or Lezgin and Ingush in the Caucasus, would be somehow protected out of a sense of solidarity among the members of the dominant (titular) nation with all those people formerly oppressed by the tsar (as that dominant ethnic group itself had been). It was a rather idealistic reading of the ethnic situation on the ground, but

Austrian prisoners of war in Russian captivity in 1915.

163

however that may be, the concept of the later Socialist Soviet republics seems to make its appearance in embryo here.

Finally, it should be underlined that both in the Habsburg and Romanov empires economic growth was unprecedently strong in the last half century before the outbreak of the First World War.[6] Profound economic change might be risky, for it precipitates social change such as urbanization, or a growing middle and working class, and so on, but it also offers the possibility that people might become stronger stakeholders of their empires, as they acquire an unheard of amount of property or a standard of living unknown to their ancestors. People might grumble about certain injustices, but it takes a leap of faith to jeopardize everything and join the revolution. In other words, were it not for the outbreak of war in 1914, and its gruesome unfolding subsequently, both empires might have survived for quite a while.

Whereas the First World War was the war that ended all empires east of the Rhine river, skilled political operators such as the Communist leaders Lenin and Stalin managed to restore a multinational empire of which the administrative language and culture were Russian. Rather than renewing Russification, they returned to a careful policy of compromises with the non-Russian nations of the Soviet Union, which in many ways was a winning strategy even if it, too, ultimately succumbed to nationalism in 1991. But much of that nationalism was forged by the Soviet Union itself.

12
The Soviet Union as Empire, 1917–91

The First World War put paid to all of Europe's empires located to the east of France.[1] Violent conflict followed this implosion everywhere, which was by far the worst in the former Russia empire, where a civil war broke out. But even if the ex-tsar's realm descended into utter chaos after its collapse, a sort of warped version of a new Russian empire arose out of the ashes of that of the Romanovs. In many ways, this polity hardly resembled its predecessor, but its language was Russian, and its leaders consisted of Russians and people acculturated as Russians. The Soviet leaders tried for about fifteen years to deny this Russian essence, but then ever more emphatically embraced it.[2]

When they began to piece back the empire, the Soviet leadership, and especially the People's Commissar of Nationalities (*narkomnats*), Stalin, showed a keen awareness of the tried-and-true method of divide and conquer that underscored so many colonial empires.[3] The Communists, like other anti-Romanov political parties, had been happy in depicting the tsarist empire as a 'prisonhouse of nations', but they proceeded to make a mockery of their initial promise of self-determination for the peoples of the Russian empire, one of the key slogans which they propagated shortly after coming to power in October 1917.[4]

Fate or luck was ultimately on the side of the Communists. Their power grab was a gamble, even if no one else seemed to know how to lead Russia after the tsar abdicated in March 1917. Lenin bluffed it in suggesting that he could lead and proved a supreme opportunist not just in taking but in keeping power after October 1917. The survival of his regime hung by a thread in February 1918, when the armed forces of the Central Powers (Germany and Austria-Hungary as well as Turkey) resumed their advance into Russian territory, once they determined that the Communists were trying to toy with them at the peace negotiations that had begun in November 1917. Ultimately, Lenin persuaded enough of his fellow leaders to accept whichever conditions the Central Powers wanted to impose, arguing that survival as Communist rulers even of a country which was as small as the Muscovy of Aleksei Mikhailovich in 1645 was worth their while. At Brest-Litovsk in early March 1918, therefore, the First World War on its easternmost European front concluded with a peace that cost Communist Russia Finland, the Baltic countries, Poland, Ukraine and part of the Caucasus.

If the Germans had been able to press their advantage on the western front (which they almost did in the spring of 1918) and won the war, Russia might have ceased to exist as an empire, with its rump becoming a sort of Russian nation-state. For, apart from the European losses that the Brest-Litovsk treaty imposed, the Soviets had no control over much of Central Asia. In its most populated region, with the Ferghana Valley its epicentre, a rebellion against the tsarist regime had broken out in 1916, as we saw previously. The Uzbeks and Tajiks protested the Russian attempt to introduce general conscription, and, when the revolution broke out in European Russia in 1917, large stretches of Central Asia were no longer under Russian control. The Soviets only gained full control over this territory in the mid-1920s.

The Germans and their allies, however, surrendered to the Western Allies in the autumn of 1918. The armistice ending the First World War in most of Europe occurred right at the time that a civil war engulfed the former Romanov empire. In broad terms, the conflict pitted Reds (Communists) versus Whites (anti-Communists). The latter besieged the centrally situated Communists from peripheral areas of the former tsarist empire, including Ukraine and the Baltic countries (from which the German military withdrew). Whereas the Reds coordinated their defence over a continuous territory, the Whites communicated with each other only with great difficulty, because the various parts from which they operated were geographically far apart. Rather than starting their offensives simultaneously and thus spreading the Red Army too thinly along the various fronts, White attacks occurred successively, making it possible for the Communist army, with the use of trains on a railway grid that allowed for relatively fast troop movement, to pick off one opponent at a time.

Compounding their uncoordinated military strategy, the Whites did not do themselves any favours by merely offering the stale slogan of a 'Russia, One and Undivided' as their political platform. The very phrase seemed to look back at the Romanov empire rather than forward to a reconstituted empire of equal nations, as the Communists seemed to offer.

In addition, the Whites accepted foreign assistance from the Allies. The Western Entente initially offered this aid in an attempt to restart the war against the Central Powers on the eastern front. After the armistice of November 1918, the British, French, Americans and Japanese continued to support the Whites in their conflict with Lenin's regime because, in their eyes, the Communists deserved punishment. Lenin's Bolsheviks were seen as having been aiders and abetters of the Central Powers, while, in addition, their communist ideology loudly threatened the future of capitalism (and Lenin's government refused to pay back the loans the tsar's government had incurred in the West). But Western and Japanese support for the Whites, which was far from wholehearted because of an immense war-weariness, may have been more harmful than beneficial: in Communist propaganda, the Whites were painted as being in league with predatory foreigners. As a result, doubt spread that the Whites had the best interests of their country at heart.

Indeed, above all, Lenin's coup had been undertaken in the name of a new world of equality and justice, which would supersede global capitalism. Communism would become the reigning philosophy of the entire planet, and international borders would become things of the past. When, by the end of 1919, they had staved off the worst attacks in the civil war and their Red Army had gained control over a significant chunk of the former tsarist realm, the Soviet leaders could begin to think about the political organization of their new country, the kernel of what was ultimately to become a global communist empire.[5] Lenin and his comrades – besides Stalin, Lev Trotsky (1879–1940) was prominent – set up an international organization of Communist parties in 1919, the *Comintern*. This was to coordinate the communist advance across the globe, but it did not really become the governing body of the communist world, as Lenin had no patience for anyone who might question his wisdom. After its second congress in 1921, it rather served the Russian Communists as an obedient tool. It was indeed Lenin's

Party that called the shots regarding anything significant in Soviet foreign and domestic policy.

This All-Union Communist Party ruled the Union of Socialist Soviet Republics (USSR). The Communist Party's leading body was its Central Committee, around 1920 consisting of a few dozen prominent members, but this small board was, too, made to bend to the will of its even much smaller executive organ, the *Politburo*. From its premises in Moscow's Kremlin, to which the government had relocated in the spring of 1918, the Politburo was to decide the fate of tens and even hundreds of millions from the early 1920s to 1991. Its five-to-ten men (women never became members with full voting rights), then, also developed the plan for the Russian empire *redux* that was the Soviet Union. Once he withdrew from his activities as a high-ranking political commissar at several civil-war fronts (as well as during the 1920–21 war with Poland), Politburo member Stalin, who was from October 1917 the People's Commissar of Nationalities in the official Soviet government (Council of People's Commissars, or *Sovnarkom*), developed the blueprint for the federal organization of the Soviet Union.

Which region should be included into the new Soviet empire, and which should be left out, was a consequence of military circumstances. The Soviet Union, initially, was considerably smaller in size than its tsarist predecessor. Poland, Finland, Estonia, Latvia and Lithuania were shed as those countries resisted Red Army occupation, while Bessarabia (northern Moldavia) was claimed by Romania. After a see-saw military conflict, Poland was able to incorporate a significant part of western Ukraine and Belarus under the terms of the Treaty of Riga that ended the Polish-Soviet war in 1921. In 1920 and 1921, the Red Army did succeed in occupying the Caucasus and Transcaucasus regions (Georgia, Armenia and Azerbaijan), which had separated from the former tsarist empire in the wake of Brest-Litovsk in 1918.

While the Basmachi revolt in Central Asia smouldered until 1925, the rest of the territory previously ruled by the Romanovs was under Soviet-Russian control by 1922, after extensive campaigning by the Red Army. The foreign power remaining the longest in the former Russian empire as part of the Allied intervention that began in 1918, Japan, withdrew from eastern Siberia in 1922. Oddly (Outer) Mongolia, which with Soviet military aid had established full independence from China in 1921, remained outside of the borders of the Soviet Union Stalin began to draw in 1921.

Georgian woman on the Mugan steppe south of the Caucasus, 1910s.

Armenian woman, *c.* 1910.

Azeri men in the 1910s near the Caspian Sea.

Faithfully following communist convictions, the Soviet empire Stalin conceived was to be based on the idea of the equality of all its ethnic communities. Formally, it was first founded by a treaty between four republics in 1922, with its organization further enshrined by the 1924 Soviet constitution.[6] These republics had, allegedly, voluntarily joined the Soviet Union, and in principle could leave this union if they chose to do so. Within those union republics, smaller territories (autonomous republics, autonomous regions, national districts) were established in which ethnic communities that did not belong to the titular nation of the larger polity received – like each of the leading nations of the union republics – their own local government and far-reaching autonomous rights regarding education, cultural expression including printing presses and theatres, and so on. One of the chambers of the bicameral legislature of the entire country was to consist of representatives of all of its territorial units. In this Soviet of Nationalities, as it was called, the larger ethnic groups were even under-represented to ensure emphatically that the voices of the minority communities were heard.

But as both Richard Pipes and Terry Martin have suggested, in terms of genuine self-determination the constitution promised far more than it delivered.[7] No doubt, non-Russians for the first time took advantage of the opportunity to send their children to schools that taught a curriculum in their mother tongue, to read printed works in their own language, and to attend plays performed in it.[8] But decisions that truly mattered, or cost significant money, were made in Moscow. The Central Executive Committee (CEC, later called Supreme Soviet), the equivalent of a Western-style bicameral parliament, both introduced legislation and chose the Sovnarkom (eventually called Council of Ministers, or *Sovmin*); the CEC chairman was formally the Soviet head of state. In reality, the Sovnarkom draughted most bills, which were then accepted by the Central Executive Committee, usually without much, or any, discussion. And whereas the CEC was to hold the Sovnarkom accountable for its policies, it did no such thing in practice.

For behind the scenes of this elaborate legislative and executive edifice operated the Central Committee and Politburo of the Communist Party of the Soviet Union. Nothing about the Party's role was said in any Soviet constitution before 1977, but it was the institution that truly ruled the Soviet Union. The Party was culturally solidly Russian, and its highest bodies, like the the CEC and the Sovnarkom, all gathered in Moscow. The Soviet head of state usually sat on the Politburo, as did several of the key People's Commissars, including its council's chairman.

The power of Stalin in the 1930s and '40s was above all based on his control over this Party apparatus, of which he was the first, or general, secretary. The Politburo made all the key appointments throughout both the Party and state bureaucracies, after which such appointments were rubber-stamped by lower-level Party or state bodies. Hundreds of such posts fell within what was called, using a slightly odd loanword, the *nomenklatura* of the Politburo.[9] Candidates for high posts were carefully vetted by the Central Committee Secretariat's personnel office, usually run by one of Stalin's most trusted minions.

Thus, whereas on paper the Soviet Union was a federalized state of equal nations, it was in truth a highly centralized empire. Far more than under the tsar, key decisions were made centrally (under Stalin, the Politburo looked at some 3,000 issues per year), and then formalized as Sovnarkom or CEC decisions. A sustained effort was made to impose a uniform ruling system everywhere across the Soviet Union. The Politburo headed a Communist Party that ballooned from about one-quarter of a million members in October 1917 to some 20 million by the time of its demise. In military style, these Communists were all to obey unconditionally their superiors in the Party organization. Telephone and radio, railway, air and car transport made it more feasible to control even the furthest reaches of the empire, even if genuine *totalitarian* control by the Kremlin remained far off, as it was hindered by insufficient technological and financial means to establish a truly adequate infrastructure necessary to exert firm control over all of this vast empire.

Meanwhile, only the highest leaders who gathered in the Politburo exerted control over an elaborate secret police apparatus, which kept everyone as much as possible under close surveillance. 'Subversives' were weeded out, with the worst offenders executed and others disappearing into the various jails and camps (and eventually psychiatric hospitals) of a brutal penal system. Informants, sometimes voluntarily, but more often coerced, denounced alleged opponents of the regime to the secret police.

The foundation of the federal Soviet Union reflected an uneasy compromise between Marxism and imperialism. According to Marx's ideology, in the communist world of the future nationalism would be a relic of the past. Nationalism reflected the global capitalist competition among the bourgeoisie (middle class) of the leading nation-states, the penultimate phase within the course of history that Marx believed he had discovered. Capitalism – and thus nationalism – would ultimately succumb to a worldwide revolution won by the proletariat (industrial working class), after which communism would triumph. Lenin suggested in 1916 that the final stage of the bourgeois phase of history was expressed in imperialism, and he implied that the First World War might be the expression of this rivalry.[10] The nationalist conflict of which imperialism was the ultimate expression would turn into a global class war. Lenin subsequently argued that the Russian communist revolution of 1917 was the first sign that the international conflict between imperialist states was giving way to the violent global class conflict that would lead to a global communist society of ultimate freedom and equality.

Yet, in the Soviet Union, cosmopolitan or supranational Soviet Man or Woman did not readily appear. For the time being, a 'Friendship of the Peoples' (*druzhba narodov*) needed to be maintained, to stave off calls for the creation of wholly independent nation-states by the various Soviet nationalities.[11] The explanation for the lingering strength of nationalist sentiments in the minds of the various Soviet peoples was that the relics, or remnants, of the past in people's thinking could not be eradicated overnight: consciousness lagged behind changes in material conditions, to express it in Marxist terms. The continued adherence to religion was another such lingering remnant.

As People's Commissar of Nationalities, Stalin recognized the tenacity of nationalism, and a hidden agenda behind the Soviet Union's foundation seems to have been the forging of an empire that would eventually be in all key respects Russified; a sort of creeping Russification would slowly wear away national allegiance.[12] This clashed with the official policy of *korenizatsiia*, which kept up the pretence that the

Soviet state accommodated and stimulated the preservation and development of national cultures, through support for education and cultural expression in non-Russian languages. After 1929, however, when Stalin was no longer encumbered by the cautionary check of some of his 1920s rivals, he implemented a crackdown on 'bourgeois-nationalist deviations' everywhere.

In Ukraine, even today Russian nationalism is seen as a key cause of the *Holomodor*, the devastating famine of 1932–3. Ukrainian nationalists argue that the confiscation of virtually all of the grain produced by Ukrainian collective farmers was conducted by Soviet officials with a twofold purpose: to ensure the food supply of the cities (and even to continue grain exports in order to pay for the importation of foreign technology and know-how), and to bridle Ukrainian nationalism. In this reading, Stalin, undoubtedly a morbidly suspicious man, became convinced that Ukrainians, out of anti-Russian and anti-Soviet spite, deliberately hoarded grain to sabotage his modernization plans of collective farming and rapid industrialization.

It very likely did indeed play a role that Stalin suspected Ukrainians – most of them still peasants rather than industrial workers – of being anti-Soviet and 'backwardly' nationalistic, while Russians were more prone to subscribe to 'forward-looking' internationalism. In some ways, though, this argument is problematic. In 1932 and 1933 it was not only the Ukrainian countryside that was robbed blind, but neighbouring Russian regions such as the Kuban, Stavropol and elsewhere, too, saw their crops confiscated by Soviet officials. And a quarter of the Kazakh population may have died in a brutal campaign that raged at the same time. Grain yields in Kazakhstan were extremely low because the Kazakhs, traditionally peripatetic herders, had been forced to settle in collective farms to grow crops, knowing next to nothing about crop tillage, and made to meet absurdly high production targets.

Even though the 1932 to 1933 onslaught was not a strictly anti-Ukrainian campaign, it appears more than evident from other policies that Stalin had lost patience by then with overly assertive expressions of non-Russian national sentiment. It seems far from coincidental that at the very time of the famines of 1932–3 a far greater emphasis on the great accomplishments of Russian culture began to be made in public discourse. The Russian language was more strongly privileged over non-Russian tongues, and non-Russian nationalist cultural policy was de-emphasized. In the Great Terror of 1936–8, Communist leaders in non-Russian areas who had been too closely associated with programmes of national-cultural development were killed. They were more often than not replaced with Russians, or non-Russians who were acculturated as Russians. From the 1930s onward, everywhere in the non-Russian republics Russians settled in far greater numbers than ever before. They were active in a variety of roles, as Party and state administrators, military and secret police personnel, industrial managers, engineers and workers, and even as collective farmers. And it had already been obvious before 1930 that those who wanted to make a career in the Soviet Union needed to become fluent in the Russian language. If they learned any second language, non-Russians learned Russian. By 1940 the cultural imperialism of the Soviet Union's Russification was in full swing.

While the collectivization of agriculture that ended most individual farming in the Soviet Union during 1929 and 1930 can be read as an autocratic move by Stalin as a sort of red tsar that did not change much about the characteristics of the Soviet Union as an empire of formally equal nations, it did contribute to the spread of a common imperial identity. The collective farms (*kolkhozy*) did make 'peasants into Soviets' (to adopt Eugen Weber's aphorism about the French). All of a sudden, peasant children everywhere went to school, villagers celebrated Soviet instead of Orthodox or Muslim holidays, the radio and films shown by itinerant movie operators kept rural dwellers abreast of the communist project's progress, libraries offered carefully vetted reading material, while Party activists and government officials gave lectures on political and non-political topics. Every few years, all participated in the elections for various government bodies at various levels: district or town, republic, all-Union. In other words, even in the countryside Soviet people became much more true, self-conscious members of an empire than they or their ancestors had ever been before. And it should be remembered that even before 1929, as a result of the multi-year military training that was part of general conscription, most young men became aware of being part of the Soviet Union's much bigger world outside of their ancestral communities.

Ultimately, the attraction of the cities became so strong that few wanted to remain behind in the countryside, pushed out as well by the unreasonable demands placed by the Soviet regime on the collective farms. The pay for collective farm work was much poorer than for almost any city job, or for jobs in the government administration in the towns or in the villages. Bereft of electricity, running water, sewers and many other modern amenities, especially younger collective-farm workers left for the city, until by the 1980s most villages had entirely emptied out.

In the cities, people were more easily swayed by the regime's imperial narrative. But even there a true belief in the radiant future of communism was undermined by the absolute brutality of the Soviet present, especially in the 1930s. Collectivization and the famine probably cost 7 or 8 million people their lives. And those ghastly chapters were followed by the Great Terror, which saw well-nigh 700,000 people executed within approximately eighteen months, demonized as 'enemies of the people', 'wreckers', 'white-guardists', 'terrorists', 'trotskyites', 'bourgeois-nationalists', 'right-deviationists', 'mensheviks', 'zinovievites', or as members of still other categories of 'counter-revolutionaries' and 'anti-Soviet elements'. Further millions were either sent to the concentration camps of the Gulag Archipelago (which was, as a veritable prison *empire*, a sort of anti-Soviet world), or, in a kind of prophylactic move, deported as members of allegedly treasonous nationalities from border areas – Koreans from eastern Siberia, Finns and Estonians from Leningrad (St Petersburg),

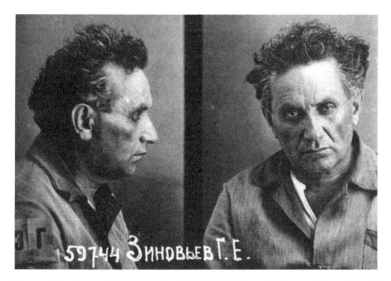

Former Leningrad Communist chief G. E. Zinoviev's mugshots of 1936.

and so on – to faraway regions.[13] Conducted by the secret police, this was political persecution on an industrial scale. It showed the immense power of the modern, twentieth-century colossus that was the Soviet Union, wielding might to transform an empire that would have been beyond the wildest dreams of the tsars.

The effect of these 'purges' on the minds of those who remained at liberty is hard to assess. Did they strengthen their sense of belonging to an empire? In 1937 and 1938, mass meetings in factories and institutions or on collective farms were staged that condemned the alleged ringleaders of all those 'alien' elements. The fervour expressed in these meetings was often genuine, but it is moot whether these 'two minutes of hate' were rooted in fear of or enthusiasm for merciless Soviet justice. The secret police and its informers kept a close watch.

In hindsight, Stalin's right-hand man Vyacheslav Molotov (1890–1986) linked the unleashing of the Great Terror to the ultimate victory over the Nazis in the Second World War, suggesting that it had rooted out most potential Soviet traitors in timely fashion.[14] But it is odd, then, that by Stalin's own admittance many Soviet inhabitants did betray their country's cause after 22 June 1941. In his wartime proclamations, many of those soldiers who had surrendered to the Nazis in the first eighteen months of the war (in often hopeless circumstances) were depicted as traitors. It seems also clear that a good number of civilians initially welcomed the Nazi-led forces as liberators, because of the brutal oppression to which many of Stalin's subjects had been exposed in exactly such episodes as the Great Terror and other instances of Soviet savagery.

The Great Terror also wiped out a substantial number of the more experienced senior Red Army officers, all the way up to some of its marshals, which handicapped the Soviet fighting capacity in 1941 and 1942. This cull was the result of a sustained fear of 'Bonapartism' among the Soviet leaders such as Stalin, who besides their Marxist immersion were usually deeply steeped in knowledge of that other great revolution in modern history, which had ended with Bonaparte's military dictatorship in 1799. When he was sidelined during the 1920s, Trotsky was tainted with the brush of wanting to be another Napoléon, because of his role as key organizer of the Red Army in the civil war and as People's Commissar of Defence until 1925. Marshal Mikhail Tukhachevsky (1893–1937), until 1937 Assistant People's Commissar of Defence and a theoretician of modern tank warfare, was butchered in the Red Army purges on accusations that he was planning a military coup together with allies in the military leadership. Even after the Second World War, in 1957, Nikita Khrushchev (1894–1971) would oust Georgii Zhukov (1896–1974) as Minister of Defence on accusations of 'Bonapartism'.

While these accusations were spurious, they are a clear sign of one specific trait in the imperial self-image of the Soviet elite. Theirs was an empire that went far beyond the historical significance of most others in history, the epicentre of a new historical era, destined, very much like the French revolutionary and Napoleonic armies, to bring the blessings of the Russian Revolution to Europe and elsewhere. The international class conflict was a violent affair, and, inevitably, the armed forces had to play – and did play in both the civil war and Second World War – a key role in achieving Communist victory. Buoyant pride in its armed forces became a hallmark of the Soviet leadership, and, certainly after the stunning victory over Hitler, of much of the Soviet population. This pride, in today's Russian Federation, survived the 1991 collapse, though much less so, of course, in the non-Russian successor states.

In the Soviet era, however, such pride was accompanied by a flipside: a paranoid fear of military dictatorship that may have been additionally rooted in a certain pacifist strain in Marxism, or in socialism in general, as can be seen in the Russian writer Leo Tolstoy's (1828–1910) convictions at the end of his life. Perhaps this was, too, the legacy of the struggle with various wannabe military dictators who had tried to overthrow the Communist regime in the civil war, such as the White commanders Alexander Kolchak (1874–1920), Anton Denikin (1872–1947, or Pyotr Wrangel (1878–1928).

This militaristic slant, meanwhile, appears to be part of a continuity in Russian history: although the various Russian

The writer L. N. Tolstoy in 1908.

(or Soviet) empires were (are) very different beasts, all three or four empires were (are) extraordinarily reliant on their army (and often, navy). Indeed, the main drive or focus of government policy was almost always geared towards the maintenance of a robust military. While such a militaristic penchant was rooted in the virtually continual foreign threat to which the Russian and Soviet empires were exposed (see Chapter Two), it might be pondered whether such a trait is unique to the Russian iterations of empire. The Roman Empire was a similarly militarily-driven enterprise, as were the gunpowder empires in early modern Asia such as those of Qing China or Moghul India. The creation of empire through persuasive, peaceful argument (or marriage, as was to some extent true for the Habsburg empire) is a rare phenomenon in history: most often an empire is built by violent means.

It is interesting in this regard to consider a possible link between the comparatively neglected state of the Russian Federation's military (as exemplified by sinking submarines, rusting vessels in port, or dubious performance in the field in the largely domestic conflicts in Chechnya) from about 1991 to the 2010s and the absence of any meaningful foreign threat to the country. During the last few years, a rekindled imperialist pride has been connected with a renewed attention to the build-up (and use) of Russia's military might, which in itself is informed by an increasing sense of foreign threat triggered by NATO's expansion into the Baltic countries and the Western flirtation with Ukraine and Georgia.

ON THE EVE OF THE Great Terror, a population count was conducted in the Soviet Union, the first since 1926. The census of 1937 showed a country populated by people who were far from becoming secular, for whom the truths of Marxism were replacing religious dogma.[15] Historians are not quite sure about the exact census results, as Stalin had them suppressed, and may have either ordered the destruction of the census records altogether or the cessation of any significant analysis of them, but after the fall of the Soviet Union in 1991 it did become clear that, in this 1937 count, more than half of the Soviet population declared themselves to be religious believers. In the eyes of the Communist leaders, it could not be doubted that people's allegiance to traditional religion (both Christianity and Islam) competed with their loyalty to the Soviet cause. Indeed, declaring oneself to be a believer was not without peril, as being religious had been stigmatized by the Soviet authorities since the early years of their rule. In other words, even more people may have been religious believers, but thought it wise to deny any such convictions. Stalin was incensed: the massive subsequent butchery of clergy during the Great Terror indicates that he interpreted the 1937 census results as a sign of a pervasive defiant mindset that needed to be eradicated by any means. Gentler means had apparently been ineffective in eradicating the 'opium of the people', as Marx had dubbed religion.

Meanwhile, it appears that the 1937 census's preliminary numbers showed Stalin that population growth had fallen far below his expectations. Ten per cent fewer people were counted than he wanted. Stalin found in this low population growth further evidence that his Soviet project was faltering. He had those who had organized and managed the census executed. In 1939 a new census was held, with the results embellished to ensure that Stalin would be pleased. Population numbers turned out according to expectations, while those surveyed were no longer asked about their religion.

Despite such savage measures, a wordly 'faith in empire' of a sort, or trust in the 'radiant future' of communism, never wholly replaced more traditional religious beliefs in the Soviet Union. Russians and non-Russians after the 1930s usually professed loyalty and even enthusiasm for the communist cause, but towards the end of the Soviet Union, and, obviously, afterwards, it became quite evident that many had furtively remained religious believers, including even hardened KGB (the final abbreviated name by which the Soviet secret police was known) officers. And as little as the propagation of a robust scientific-communist identity – or even brutal intimidation and persecution of religious servants – suppressed religious feelings in many Soviet citizens, as little seems identification with a supranational Soviet identity to have replaced stubborn nationalist sentiments in many people's minds.

Stalin himself seems to have realized this: even after he had allegedly rid his empire of its enemies in the Great Terror, his distrust of non-Soviet-Russian nationalism continued unabated. When in August 1939 the Molotov-Ribbentrop Pact was signed between Hitler's Third Reich and the Soviet Union, a secret clause was included that allowed the Soviets to re-incorporate most of the former tsarist empire's western territories that had been lost at Brest-Litovsk in 1918. Once the Baltic countries, western Belarus and western Ukraine were occupied by Soviet troops in 1939 and 1940, tens of thousands of people were arrested as 'bourgeois-nationalists' and either deported to the *Gulag* camps or executed. Perhaps this was still understandable from the grim logic that had become manifest in the Great Terror (and perhaps even in the 1932–3 *Holomodor* or Kazakh famine): not being part of the Soviet Union before 1939 or 1940, the residents of these newly acquired territories had not been subjected to the scrutiny of the years 1937 and 1938.

But through his subsequent actions Stalin tacitly admitted that he did not discount the continued force of nationalism within his empire – and the insufficient prophylactic cleansing of alien elements in the Great Terror in 1937 and 1938 – in 1941 and beyond. When the Nazis invaded, tens of thousands of German speakers, many of whom had lived in Ukraine and Russia since the eighteenth century, were deported to Siberia, an operation that had to be halted once the Nazi armies began to advance too swiftly and the front line neared the Soviet-German areas of settlement. German identity trumped Soviet identity, apparently. Later, during the Nazi retreat from Soviet territory, Stalin decided that entire ethno-cultural communities – Chechens, Ingushetians, Crimean Tatars, Kalmyks, Meshketian Turks and Balkars – had betrayed the Soviet Union and had the secret police deport them to Central Asia and Siberia. Such an imperial whim has been rare in history.[16] And these actions betrayed a profound fear of nationalism lurking behind them all.

The 1944–5 population exchanges in East-Central Europe, crude solutions to solve nationalist tensions, underscore how Stalin became desirous of a simplification of the ethnic map of his empire.[17] By 1944 he seems to have grudgingly concluded that the Poles could not be browbeaten into loyal Soviet subjects and that it would be best to concentrate them at least formally within their own independent nation-state. He allowed local officials and vigilantes in Ukraine and Belarus to evict Poles and other non-desirable types and send them across the new Polish borders; Poles seem to have done the same with

The Soviet Union as Empire

Ukrainians and Belarusians, and even more so with the millions of Germans who had previously lived on territory that was now made part of the post-war Polish state. Germans were also banished from Czechoslovakia, Hungary, Romania and Yugoslavia, even if they had lived for centuries all over East-Central Europe. The German-speaking communities of the Baltic countries were eradicated as well, a process that had started to a degree in the period from August 1939 to June 1941, albeit in a less violent fashion.

The ethnic hatred all of this caused was profound, and served as a lightning conductor distracting from Stalin's blunt efforts to expand his empire far beyond the Soviet international borders. An outer empire of formally independent satellites appeared on the map, which were under firm Soviet control by the time of Stalin's death in 1953. And after 1945 the Soviet Union itself encompassed a territory of almost the same size as Nicholas II's Russian empire in 1914.

Stalin's redrawing of the map of Europe was a blatant exercise in power politics that had little to do with the rules of international law as it was understood in the middle of the twentieth century. It was in clear violation of the spirit and practice of the 1945–6 Nuremberg Trials that condemned Nazism and its surviving leaders. But Stalin could do as he pleased because his Western allies had neither the will nor the means to stop him, as had become evident during the three Big Three conferences at Tehran (1943), Yalta and Potsdam (both 1945). The American president Franklin Roosevelt (1882–1945) and, to a much lesser extent, the British prime minister Winston Churchill (1874–1965), and a good chunk of public opinion in the Western world, thought that Soviet expansion was only deserved in exchange for the absurd human and material cost the Soviet Union had suffered, shouldering the lion's share of defeating the Third Reich. No one outside a select few occupants of the Kremlin knew in 1945 that the Second World War had cost the Soviet Union one-sixth of its population, but that the death toll had been enormous was clear enough from anecdotal evidence about the siege of Leningrad (1941–4) or the battle of Stalingrad (1942–3).

It is not clear how Stalin appreciated this astounding cost of war. He expressed on a few occasions, in July and November 1941 and in May and June of 1945, his gratitude for his subjects' resolute stand against the Nazi hordes. In the late spring of 1945, he especially singled out the Russians as the leading nation who had set the example in this regard (admitting thereby publicly that nationalism was not yet a spent force among the Soviet peoples). Stalin's relief about his subjects' continued loyalty to his empire might be read in such praise. But for a brief moment a few days into the war, though, he never appears to have felt guilty about the series of blunders that had left his armed forces and his people quite unprepared for the Nazi attack in June 1941, and probably should have cost him his head.[18] Given Stalin's record of bloodletting, did he think that the expansion of his empire had been worth the death of 27 million people? He likely thought that such slaughter was deplorable, but much of this loss was compensated for by his gain of an empire that was the largest history had ever seen. He appears to have comforted himself with the thought that he had overseen great progress towards the global communist triumph, perhaps setting up a springboard for its ultimate victory.

In his final years, Stalin closely watched over his empire. He realized that, whereas he needed to rebuild a good part of the Soviet economy from wartime ruin and continue to pour money into his military-industrial complex in the escalating Cold War, much remained to be done in making his underlings into convinced communists, wholehearted denizens of the unique Soviet empire that was to lead humanity to a restored Eden. Too many of his subjects were still tempted to question some parts of his project. Writers, scientists, composers, philosophers, linguists and even theatre critics were raked over the coals after 1945. Communist leaders in the East-Central European satellites were scapegoated in order to further enforce unconditional obedience to Moscow's rule in those countries. And still further ethnic groups fell under suspicion of disloyalty. Within a mere few years after the Holocaust, Stalin sanctioned the eradication of Soviet-Jewish culture. Soviet policies implied that there was no place for Jews within the Soviet Union, once Israel had proclaimed its independence in 1948. Anti-Semitic hysteria reached a feverish pitch in late 1952, only to be stopped by Stalin's death in March 1953.

Meanwhile, the Cold War seemed on the verge of turning hot around 1950. Stalin, it appears from evidence that became public after 1991, was in fact eager to avoid a third world war, as long as his country was licking its war wounds. But he was careful not to lull himself to sleep as he had done with Hitler. In 1949 Soviet scientists successfully detonated an atomic bomb, which lost the USA its nuclear monopoly. He tacitly supported Kim Il-Sung's invasion of South Korea, but only by proxy: it was newly Communist China that provided 1 million 'volunteers' who bailed out their North Korean comrades when things went awry in 1950. Soviet planes were repainted with Korean insignia and the Soviet pilots who flew them were instructed to communicate in English to hide their identity.

Stalin was remarkably muted in welcoming the victory of Mao Zedong's Communists in the Chinese civil war in 1949. Almost until the end of this conflict, Stalin refused to believe in the possibility of a Communist triumph in China, and merely offered token support. Almost betraying the cause of international Communist solidarity, he promised Mao little aid, when the latter, soon after his victory, came to Moscow in late 1949. Stalin was willing to surrender the territories of Xinjiang, Manchuria and parts of Inner Mongolia to the Chinese, in which Soviet forces had been deployed in 1945 and which they garrisoned until the end of the Chinese civil war. But Stalin, perhaps because old age and illness prevented him from developing a coherent and lucid strategy looking forward, seemed unsure what to do now that, on paper, the Communist empire encompassed one-third of the world population.

Like not a few other dictators, Stalin refused to designate or groom a successor. His towering presence dwarfed all around him. No one seemed properly equipped to succeed him upon his death in 1953. The ranking Politburo members who had stood at his side in his last years decided to divide the senior responsibilities in the Party and state leadership. Five years later, Khrushchev had emerged as the unrivalled leader, but his power was never near absolute as that of Stalin had been, and he was ousted in 1964. His successor was Leonid Brezhnev (1906–1982), who very carefully manoeuvred to become first among equals, and was wary so as not to appear as a real dictator. After Brezhnev, the Soviet empire rapidly came unstuck, precisely because Brezhnev was unwilling to challenge the brittle balance between various stakeholders within the Politburo and their retinue, such as the Party apparatus, the government, the military, the secret police, Ukraine or Kazakhstan. The

Soviet empire was in desperate need of renewal by 1970, but Brezhnev lacked the boldness of Stalin or Khrushchev, who had sought to reinvigorate the system but failed to come up with a viable plan.

From 1953 to 1985, protest was voiced against the Soviet hegemon inside the country itself, in its satellites, and in Communist China. Friendly relations with Mao did not last for more than a decade, and in 1969 armed clashes between Soviet and Chinese military units on the Ussuri river in Siberia signalled a total break. In East Germany in 1953, Poland and Hungary in 1956, Czechoslovakia in 1968, and Poland in 1970, as well as in 1980–81, widespread disaffection with Soviet rule was expressed in major protests. These rebellions were suppressed with military force (either Soviet or those of the native Communist regime), but anti-Communist hostility continued to smoulder. In the Soviet Union, after contradictory policies regarding the freedom of expression under Khrushchev, Brezhnev tried to end the 'dissident' movement, but, even if by 1980 most opponents had been silenced, apathy and resentment spread, rapidly undermining the foundation of the Soviet regime. The project of creating a new Soviet Man and Woman, a *homo sovieticus*, was entirely shelved after 1964. Instead, Soviet authorities engaged in a sort of tired persecution of organized religion or overly strong nationalist expressions. Little truly positive was offered with which people could identify.

The Soviet invasion of Afghanistan in 1979 proved a disastrous military adventure abroad. By the 1980s, it appeared that few inside or outside the Soviet Union continued to believe that communist utopia was around the corner. Certainly, some Soviet citizens still took pride in being part of a powerful empire that rivalled the West in military strength and commanded respect as one of the world's two superpowers, while being a permanent member of the United Nations' Security Council. But whereas in 1953 the further expansion of the Soviet empire seemed to be on the horizon, a generation later the implosion of the Soviet empire was imminent.

Various countries in Asia and Africa did for a while flirt with communism, but more often than not abandoned the Soviet model of development and their alliance with the Soviet Union once the yield of adopting a planned economy and joining the Soviet Bloc proved meagre. Cuba became Communist in the early 1960s, but more out of anti-American hostility than pro-Soviet conviction. Communist-led Vietnam, Yugoslavia and China began to seek other paths to economic development than through regimented development guided by overbearing central planning. In Western Europe, once formidable Communist parties melted away, as they did in France and Italy.

Great power comes with great responsibilities, the cliché goes. The post-1991 history of the Soviet successor states seems to indicate that authoritarian or dictatorial regimes can meet with considerable public approval if they provide security, stability and a decent standard of living: for example, compare the Russian indulgence in Putin's rather dubious foreign and unimaginative domestic policy to the utter chaos into which Ukraine has sunk. In Russia, life is bearable, these days: per capita income quadrupled in the 2000s, and, even after the economic boycott of 2014, stabilized at about 25,000 dollars per year; in Ukraine, where in 2017 per capita income was just over a third of that of Russia, it is unbearable for far too many.[19]

The Soviet regimes of the late Brezhnev, Yuri Andropov (1914–1984) and Konstantin Chernenko (1911–1985) years did not provide well for its citizens. Mikhail Gorbachev (b. 1932), who took the reins in March 1985, soon realized that a significant overhaul was necessary to make the Soviet empire survive. But his attempt likely came too late, as became clear fairly quickly when his slogans of *glasnost'* (openness) and *perestroika* (restructuring) began to acquire some meaningful content. This sharper reformist turn was in many ways the consequence of the unbelievably bumbling response to the Chernobyl disaster, a meltdown of a nuclear reactor that saw unprecedented amounts of radiation released into the atmosphere in April 1986. Local officials were paralysed when confronted with the disaster, while higher-ups hesitated far too long to admit to the scale of the disaster and urge swift emergency measures. Only two weeks after the disaster started did Gorbachev admit to the outside world what had occurred. It showed how the empire had become a lifeless shell, for whose survival no one seemed to feel particularly responsible.

Gorbachev subsequently tried to do the right thing by releasing incarcerated and banished dissidents (the usual name given to opponents of the Soviet regime), encouraging criticism of the Soviet past and present, withdrawing from Afghanistan, allowing the East-Central European satellites to go their own way, reintroducing small-scale private enterprise, and rewriting the Soviet constitution to make the Soviet Union a partnership of truly equal republics with a comprehensive right to self-determination. Several of the SSRs, however, refused by 1991 even to sign the new, equitable, union treaty that Gorbachev submitted to them. And for the general populace in those republics (including Russia) the stagnation and gradual decline in the standard of living became so pronounced – as well as blatant when compared with the West, a comparison which many could make now that the Western way of life began to be shown on television – that cutting the umbilical cord with the Soviet motherland seemed worth the risk that it might entail.

Finally, the unprecedented decentralization of the empire by way of the new union treaty was far too radical for many of the Communist Old Guard, who held key positions in the government in Moscow. In August 1991 Gorbachev was confined to his holiday home on their orders. But their Emergency Committee (GKChP or Gosudarstvennyi Komitet po chrezvychainomu polozheniiu, or 'State Committee for the Emergency Situation') failed to grasp that few people in the Soviet Union remained interested in preserving the Soviet empire to which this Old Guard felt loyal. Demonstrators took to the streets of Moscow and St Petersburg, as Leningrad once again began to be called. Those in uniform called in to suppress the demonstrations refused to do so. The Soviet Union had come to an end. It was officially dissolved on 1 January 1992.

13
Since 1991: *Russkii* or *Rossiiskii*?

Should Russia shed all of its *Rossiiskii* traits and become a 'pure' nation-state, ethnically and linguistically *Russkii* and shedding all the remnants of its imperial vestiges? While the peoples of the Russian Federation might be happier living in such a nation-state in theory, this may be difficult to realize in practice. For it remains an open question in how far the 'balkanization' of the Russian Federation then would need to go. The first Russian president, Boris Yeltsin (1931–2007), clearly drew a line in the sand when he refused to allow Chechnya to go its own way in the mid-1990s. And what should be the fate of the Mordovian or Komi republics, or Tatarstan along the Volga, completely landlocked and surrounded by Russian territory?

At the least, meanwhile, the memory of empire lingers, both among the population of today's Russian Federation and that of the surrounding successor states, called 'near abroad', *blizhnee zarubezh'e* in Russia.[1] Nostalgic pride in their country's past greatness affects many Russians, but pride in empire is also linked to current concerns. For example, most of the non-Russian states that appeared as independent polities on the map in early 1992 have considerable Russian-speaking minorities. Not all of those Russians in the 'near abroad' identify with the Russian Federation (which complicates the current conflict in eastern Ukraine), but within these communities the fear of discrimination because of being seen as Russian, and of the suppression of cultural institutions such as Russian schools, is widespread. In the Tiraspol area within Moldova, as early as 1992 an eastern Slavic enclave, Transnistria, was created that relied on support by the Russian military. It still today guards its borders against any Moldovan aggression. Remarkably, Russian and Ukrainians in this region found common ground in their hostility to any Romanization on the part of the Moldovans. Some even feared that Moldova might join Romania, the language of which the Moldovans speak.

Indeed, it is not just a Moscow ploy to argue that Russian minorities in non-Russian parts are sometimes persecuted. In the fallout of the Soviet collapse, a significant number of Russians fled to the Russian Federation, sometimes after being chased out by local vigilantes who acted with the connivance of their government, although the fear of becoming victims of some sort of ethnic reckoning might have been rather greater than this actually occurring.[2] And the Armenian-Azeri slaughter that started in 1988 seemed to underline the truly mortal danger of ethnic conflict.[3] Ethnic violence in the early 1990s also plagued Georgia, while tribal hatred was on renewed display in the wars in Chechnya in the mid-1990s and around 2000.[4]

As much as Russian minorities feel oppressed by the Ukrainian or Latvian governments, the governments and people of the non-Russian successor states are, not without some ground, wary of a Russian penchant for resurrecting the empire in its larger iteration as it existed before 1992. Until 2014, such fears could be dismissed as signs of paranoia, but the annexation of Crimea and the virtual independence of eastern Ukraine (and its factual submission to Russia) in that year have made clear that Russia is willing to meddle violently in countries. While the Russian motive for this armed intervention combines an exaggerated sense of responsibility to its former imperial subjects and a longing for a revivified Russian empire, one suspects that politicians in the Kremlin also counted on scoring political points with their domestic audience through the display of military might.

While such cynicism can only be condemned, there are a host of territorial disputes resulting from the sudden and ill-prepared Soviet demise that still need a legitimate resolution. It would have made sense in the 1990s to organize an exhaustive international round-table conference in which many of the details could have been hammered out regarding the successor states' exact border locations, minority rights within them, and so on. For example, Crimea, Russian-occupied since 2014, had been considered a part of the RSFSR from 1920 onward. Then the peninsula was handed over to the Ukrainian SSR in 1954. By 1992, the great majority of its population still identified as Russian rather than Ukrainian. Further historical reasons, meanwhile, complicate Crimea's case. In 1944, Stalin was miffed at alleged large-scale collaboration among the Crimean Tatars with the Nazi-led forces that had occupied the peninsula, and ordered their deportation, another ethnic cleansing before the term was coined. Hundreds of thousands of Tatars were packed on cargo trains and deported to Central Asia. After Stalin's death few were allowed to return to Crimea, even if it was tacitly admitted by the Soviet leadership that the deportations had been a crime against humanity.

Since, however, only slightly more than 10 per cent of the current Crimean population is Tatar today, would the declaration of an independent Crimean-Tatar state encompassing part of the peninsula be wise, even if it might be historically just? The hairy question of Crimea's status should probably have been immediately raised when Russia's Boris Yeltsin and Ukraine's Leonid Kravchuk (b. 1934) decided to declare the independence of their respective countries from the Soviet Union in late 1991.

Even when discounting Crimea, Ukraine today is an odd amalgam of disparate parts. We saw how one part formally became Russian in 1667, but territories west of Kyiv and the Dnipro river were added much later, with L'viv and Uzhhorod becoming a definitive part of the Ukrainian SSR only at the end of the Second World War. The case can be made for a shared Ukrainian language and culture for the majority of people living from Uzhhorod in the west to Kharkiv in the east, but beyond the latter city the situation was much less clear-cut before fighting broke out there in 2014. This violent conflict led to the self-proclaimed republics of Lugansk and Donetsk along the Don river. In them, especially after the flight of many Ukrainian speakers, the great majority of the population is Russian-speaking (which is not the same as identifying as Russian; more than 10 per cent of those identifying as Ukrainian in Ukraine are Russian speakers). Many of these people trace their arrival in the region to the late nineteenth century, when in the first wave of tsarist industrialization coal mines were established in the area, the workforce being predominantly Russian migrants.[5]

The border between southern Russia and Ukraine was only precisely demarcated under the auspices of Stalin as People's Commissar of Nationalities during the early 1920s: he more or less appears to have traced the old tsarist provincial borders to distinguish Ukraine from Russia, regardless of the fact that the Don region was populated by a mix of peoples defying any clear territorial demarcation of ethnocultural homelands. Of course, Stalin did not have to worry overly about this, as Soviet Ukraine and Soviet Russia were not to exist as independent states. But by 1991 his delineation of the borders suddenly became rather more important. Presidents Yeltsin of Russia and Kravchuk of Ukraine piously promised to respect minority rights within their new countries, but for the Russian ethnic minority (those identifying as Russian, that is) of eastern Ukraine the independence of Ukraine meant a change in status from belonging to the dominant ethnic group to a dominated ethnic group, at least in theory. The waters were subsequently further poisoned by the gradually increasing economic gap between the more prosperous Russian Federation and a stagnating Ukraine, mired in a continual economic crisis which was felt even worse in the sort of rustbelt that is the eastern Ukrainian borderlands. Many ethnic Russians longingly began to look at Russia, in hopes of better material conditions.

While in all of this neither the various Ukrainian leaders nor Presidents Putin and Dmitrii Medvedev (b. 1965) have come up with any imaginative and feasible solutions regarding the Ukrainian and Crimean situation before or after 2014, little help has been offered by others either. I previously mentioned the idea of a long-term and exhaustive international conference, to which might be added the setting up of an arbitration agency with binding powers, to resolve border and minority issues in the Soviet successor states. The West could have done much better than smugly wallow in the great triumph of capitalism and democracy, which too easily became the way in which the epochal events of the 1989 to 1991 years were interpreted. Once the dust settled, few showed much interest in any of the states into which the Soviet Union fell apart in 1991, with the exception perhaps of the Baltic states. This was different from the sustained and constructive interest in the fate of the former Soviet satellites, to whom Europe, and to some extent the United States, seemed desperate to try to make it up to for abandoning them in 1945. A more encouraging policy towards Russia (and Ukraine) during the 1990s might have prevented subsequent troubles.

Nostalgia for past greatness in Russia was inflamed when not only the European Union, but the North Atlantic Treaty Organization (NATO) expanded into formerly Soviet territory. Once Latvia and Estonia joined NATO in 2004, even Western military experts admitted that NATO's reach had suddenly neared Moscow in a disturbingly close fashion, its forces deployed within a few kilometres of Pskov, Novgorod and St Petersburg.

Meanwhile, a newly minted NATO member such as Latvia did nothing to defray Russian suspicions when it began to celebrate the feats of Latvian SS units, who had fought against the Soviet Union in the Second World War. Additionally, its government seemed to harass its large Russian minority by such things as enforcing the use of the Latvian language in government offices and educational institutions. This culturally Russian community has stayed mum about most of this badgering, because any heightened discrimination against it has to some degree been compensated by the markedly improved living conditions that followed Latvia's joining of the EU.

Imperial nostalgia combined with even greater worries in Russia once NATO and the EU seemed to start to flirt with Ukraine when under Viktor Yushchenko (president from 2005 to 2010) and with Georgia under Mikheil Saakashvili (president from 2004 to 2013). A look at the map will tell the reader that Moscow would be faced by two pincers if Ukraine was to join the Western alliance, with Ukraine situated to its south and Estonia and Latvia to its northwest. Historical wits might draw a parallel with the strategic situation of Tsar Aleksei's Muscovy in the middle of the seventeenth century. Then, similar to today, Russia was faced with strong hostile powers (Sweden and the Rzeczpospolita then, the Baltic NATO members today) on its western borders, while Ukraine, if it is embraced by the Western alliance, might be turned into the second coming of the Crimean Tatars (who, it should be remembered, were backed by the hegemonic Ottoman Empire) threatening Russia.

Regardless of any historical analogies, to have a hostile military alliance deployed in those pincers should be disturbing to Russian politicians interested in preserving their country's unfettered independence. The aggressive Russian response both to Georgia's meddling in southern Ossetia and to Ukrainian unrest provoked by the bumbling and overly pro-Russian Viktor Yanukovych (president, 2010–14) during Kyiv's *Euromaidan* of 2013–14 was partially born from this fear of being caught in a vice.

These foreign threats reinforce a longing for the time when no one dared to challenge Russia in such a bold fashion, that is, that of the Soviet Union from 1945 to 1991, and even earlier iterations of the Russian empire. Estonia and most of Latvia were under Russian control from 1721 to 1918, and again from 1945 to 1991, and eastern Ukraine since 1667. For many Russians, it seems incomprehensible that these territories may now be a launchpad for a NATO attack. For them, NATO's advance indicates a signal failure of post-Soviet foreign policy, strengthening many Russians' revulsion about the 1990s, a decade that was painful in other ways as well. Toynbee's suggestion that historically Russia has been besieged and that its expansionist moves are defensive rather than aggressive in nature will seem highly accurate to them.

It would have been preferable if NATO had found a better way to address Russian fears of any aggressive designs, especially after the Baltic countries joined it in 2004. But the real opportunity was likely missed earlier, in the 1990s, when politicians in the EU and NATO countries passed up on the chance to welcome the Russian Federation into their midst. Some feelers to ask Russia to join were apparently put out in those days, but a self-absorbed EU (partially distracted with the Yugoslavian tragedy) and a confused post-Cold-War USA ultimately missed their chance.

Still, as I suggested earlier, foreign threats may be exaggerated for domestic consumption, forcing the population to follow the flag at a time when the motherland is once again in peril. Military adventures such as in Crimea or eastern Ukraine seem at least in part to be inspired by the idea that this may lead to a surge in patriotic pride among the Russians. Putin's leadership has often lacked imagination in trying to win the Russians to support him. Rather than solving the numerous profound and hard-to-solve problems that affect the Russian Federation – such as environmental destruction, the poor state of housing or infrastructure, the highly unequal distribution of wealth, and so on – drummed-up nationalism is a fallback strategy used by politicians everywhere to gain and maintain popular support.

A few words need to be further said about the recent fate of the many non-Russian peoples that still reside in the Russian

Federation, whose fate was referred to in the opening paragraph of this chapter. For, despite the reduction of Russia to the size of late Muscovy, the Russian Federation still harbours sizable ethnocultural minorities. Indeed, one of them, that of the Chechens, seemed poised to break off from Russia in the later 1990s. The Chechen conflict ended through the use of brutal force, which may have served as a deterrent to other non-Russian ethnocultural communities to attempt to establish greater independence from the Russian republic. For most of these minorities today, accommodation with the Russian state seems the saner route to take, as they reside in territories surrounded by ethnic Russian areas, or live in areas where ethnic Russians form a large minority, or even a majority, as is the case in parts of the Komi or Mordovian republics, for example.

Ultimately, most non-Russians in the Russian Federation are becoming more and more acculturated to its dominant culture, in part because this presents them with better economic options: the number of Tatar speakers, for example, has been dropping quite significantly according to the most recent censuses held in the Russian Federation. Refusing to assimilate and holding to one's traditional way of life becomes less and less feasible as well for many people because of the encroachment on the lands of native communities by industry and mining.[6] Russians' concern for the environment is as fickle as it is in the Western world; once in a while, environmental protection or restoration is undertaken, but only if it does not interfere with the mining or processing of ore, or the winning of gas and oil.

In the light of such advancing Russification (and the spectre of another Chechnya), a falling apart of the Russian Federation, which was sometimes predicted in the 1990s, seems unlikely in the foreseeable future. Even the Japanese claims on the Kurile islands or southern Sakhalin are routinely dismissed without much thought (and against a Japan that is militarily weak). After the disastrous international response to the Crimean and eastern Ukrainian meddling, any sustained attempts at renewed expansion seem as unlikely. Indeed, it remains unclear if the Crimean annexation will ever be recognized by the international community.

Perhaps somewhere during the twenty-first century Russia will have to face a more aggressive China, which can mount historical claims to Siberia. Its vast natural resources might fuel Chinese manufacturing, while its immense space might provide room for the Chinese population, nowadays ten times as large as that of Russia. But this is probably groundless speculation, given the trajectory of China's rather successful 'economic imperialism' of the early decades of this century. A sort of symbiosis of a Russia producing the raw materials for China's vast manufacturing sector might be a more likely outcome. A significant part of a pipeline pumping natural gas from Russian fields to China was completed in late 2019.

Certainly, even if much reduced in international status since 1991, the Russian Federation remains a considerable power, even when its GDP is less than half that of Germany. Strengths other than economic heft aim to underline that might. At home and abroad, the mastermind of sowing confusion by mixing up fake news with real information has been Vladislav Surkov, one of Vladimir Putin's closest advisors since before the beginning of Putin's presidency in 2000. The nefarious recent efforts to destabilize a number of countries by interfering in their elections through computer and other manipulation are probably the most crass examples of strategies that aim to increase

Russia's power and influence by means other than military or economic. In the reading of the Putin government, Russia's international clout increases if the resolve and unity of, for example, NATO or the European Union, weaken: causing turmoil within the member states of those organizations and supporting forces that are anti-EU or anti-NATO is therefore in the Russian interest. It is to be deplored that the alternative, strengthening Russia through more intense and amicable international collaboration, was so quickly abandoned after the early days of Putin's presidency.

More directly, the Russian Federation has been involved in a rather dubious role during the Syrian conflict, allowing the murderous Assad regime to recover from the brink of defeat. It has taken a more positive part in resolving the worst of the tension between the West and Iran, and plays an important role in Central Asia, which, apart from the plentiful fossil fuels some of its countries harbour, is too often neglected by the rest of the world. Economically, Russia has recovered from the disastrous 1990s, and despite the hostility that Russian interference in Ukrainian affairs has generated, remains a close trading partner of both China and the EU, attesting to its undeniably important economic role internationally despite its modest GDP. The European Union can ill afford to lose access to Russian natural gas and several other 'strategic' resources that Russia exports, such as nickel, gold or diamonds. And Russia remains a permanent member of the United Nations' Security Council, which means it has veto-right regarding the solution of any key international dispute through the UN. Lastly, it has the world's second largest nuclear arsenal, and a vast conventional armed force to boot.

Afterword: Is the Age of Political Empires Over?

Not merely Russians stand today in awe of the amazing tenacity, or endurance, of the Russian empire. For casual observers (and wishful thinkers), it seems that, besides perhaps Rome, Egypt or China, only Russia has survived this long, a whole millennium, as a vast empire. But, as I have argued, such a superficial perception ignores the tenuous linkage between Kyivan Rus' and Muscovy, or Muscovy and today's Russian Federation. It seems to show how the lure of a glorious eternal empire is strong, even if its existence is a chimera.

Both lingering imperial and nationalist ideology cannot readily accept that one's *patria* is just a country like the next. If anyone doubts this, observing the tortuous road towards Brexit in the United Kingdom may be enlightening: in many ways, as seems evident from the UK's entire history with the EEC and EU, the enthusiasm for this foolhardy scheme is embedded in imperialist nostalgia. Especially many English (rather than Scottish) people have yet to come to terms with the end of the British Empire, and believe somehow that the days of splendid Albion are not yet past or might return. Opportunistic politicians such as Vladimir Putin or Boris Johnson (b. 1964) capitalize on this sentiment, often implying that empire equals prosperity and happiness, even if the opposite of this seems to be true: there is not a shadow of a doubt that the UK is better off today than it would have been if it had rejected the EU in 1973, even if its standard of living has improved comparatively less than that of Spain, Estonia or Ireland after they joined the EU. Russia, though in much better economic shape than in 1991, should probably be better off, if it had been consistently led by truly visionary politicians.

In the Russian case, alas, the imperial legacy and imperialist attitudes have never been quite discarded among those who make the country's key decisions, or, to be exact, seem to have merely been suspended briefly, from late 1991 to the beginning of the first Chechen War in late 1994. An enormous military has been maintained, and conscription, which means many months of military service even without further mobilization, still exists. Nuclear arms and other sophisticated weaponry such as submarines, aircraft carriers and aeroplanes are not exactly cheap. Russia already faces the challenge of having to staff a vast army of border guards because of its lengthy frontier. Having to keep alive a huge military to enable the government to engage in sabre-rattling (and worse) adds enormously to government expenditure. While one may argue that the military provides a key stimulus that keeps the manufacturing sector and other branches of the Russian economy afloat, it does seem that if the money had been spent otherwise, the Russian standard of living might be much higher, and the still considerable incidence of poverty in the country might have been significantly alleviated. Indeed, one only has to look at the neighbouring EU, which spends very little on defence, to argue for a nexus between higher standards of living and lower military expenditure by the government.

Theoreticians like Miroslav Hroch, Benedict Anderson or Eric Hobsbawm have rightfully suggested that mass nationalism is a modern phenomenon. Before the nineteenth century, nonetheless, a sense of imperial and national identity, or belonging, may be discerned among the middle and upper classes, or strata, and even among broader layers of the population, in many polities in Europe and elsewhere, beginning with Spartan soldiers and Athenian citizens and expressed in the term *Senatus Populusque Romanus*, the SPQR written on the standards the Roman legions carried around on their wars of conquest. It often was, or is, mixed up with a measure of religion, including a belief in a monarch with semi-divine traits, and there is no denying that belief in one's empire or nation was, or is, motivated by a certain degree of self-interest, as support for the imperial project was and is sometimes rewarded with spoils. Such was the case at least for the Russian elite, its noble warriors and those who made a career thanks to the Table of Ranks.

After 1789, in a process akin to that described by Norbert Elias regarding the percolation of 'civilized manners' from high (especially in the case of Louis XIV's court) to low across Europe, faith in nation, or empire, descended upon ever broader layers of society in an accelerated process thanks to modern means of communication, ever greater levels of literacy, the declining power of churches to command the attention and loyalty of their flocks, and outright government propaganda in education and army training.[1] This process took only a few generations in most European states. Russia was once again no exception to this, even if in Russia the spread of nationalism among the Russians was far from complete by 1914.

On the eve of the First World War, as Lenin cuttingly observed, the working class of the European Powers had in a sense become the exploiters of the downtrodden elsewhere in the world.[2] Its growing prosperity came at the price of the growing exploitation of the peons in the overseas (or in the Russian case, adjacent) colonies. And pride in nation was often wholly entangled with pride in empire among the working class in the United Kingdom, Germany and France, and among the German-speaking lower classes of Austria-Hungary as well as the Russian masses in the tsar's empire.

Such imperial pride, at least in the Russian case, spread further during the Soviet years, and endures today in the Russian Federation. It may have worn a little thin in the darkest days of the post-Soviet era during the 1990s, but it has made a come-back in recent years: it is moot, however, how deeply such a longing for empire is anchored in people's minds, and how much it is truly a mass phenomenon. It remains to be seen, too, whether this sentiment is a harbinger of an actual return of an imperial, rather than an imperious, Russia.

References

Preface

1 Readers may object that this book does not discuss the Ukrainian Hetmanate as one of these polities; although such an argument has merit, the Hetmanate was hardly ever recognized as an independent state, while it never aspired to be an empire.
2 H. White, 'Foucault Decoded: Notes from Underground', *History and Theory*, XII/1 (1973), pp. 23–54, p. 28; Michel Foucault, *The Order of Things: Introduction to the Archeology of Human Sciences* (New York, 1970). Foucault himself is not easy to read or interpret, but in 'Foucault Decoded' Hayden White has rendered a lucid explication of this work.
3 See Philip Longworth, *Russia: The Once and Future Empire from Pre-history to Putin* (New York, 2005), p. 319, and *passim*.
4 Longworth reserved judgement regarding the post-Soviet period; perhaps it is still too early to say with any confidence whether Putin's Russia represents a transition phase rather than a distinct historical epoch, but I will provisionally include it as a fifth incarnation of a significant Russian state, although I doubt that it is once again an empire.
5 The most lucid and sober discussion of this is undoubtedly Plokhy's: see Serhii Plokhy, *The Origins of the Slavic Nations: Premodern Identities in Russia, Ukraine, and Belarus* (Cambridge, 2006), pp. 10–84.
6 Best work on this period is Chester Dunning, *Russia's First Civil War: The Time of Troubles and the Founding of the Romanov Dynasty* (University Park, PA, 2001).
7 Besides Longworth, a fine work 'taking the long view' is V. A. Kivelson and R. G. Suny, *Russia's Empires* (Oxford, 2016).

Worthwhile as well is Geoffrey Hosking, *Russia: People and Empire* (Cambridge, MA, 1997).
8 Paul Kennedy, *The Rise and Fall of the Great Powers: Economic Change and Military Conflict from 1500 to 2000* (New York, 1987).

1 Empire, Imperial Identity and Colonial Rule: The Russian Case

1 Krishan Kumar, *Visions of Empire: How Five Imperial Regimes Shaped the World* (Princeton, NJ, 2017). It, of course, is in itself a myth, beginning with its thousand-year existence, to which the Nazis referred. See as well Rudi Matthee, 'Was Safavid Iran an Empire?', *Journal of the Economic and Social History of the Orient*, LIII/1–2 (2010), pp. 233–65.
2 It was resurrected more than three hundred years later by Charlemagne (742–814) in 800, but after his death led an anaemic existence, until it acquired renewed prestige thanks to the teamwork (despite their loud conflicts) of pope and emperor in the time of the Salian emperors (1027–1125).
3 See James Billington, *The Icon and the Axe: An Interpretive History of Russian Culture* (New York, 1966); and Mikhail Cherniavsky, '*Khan* or *Basileus*: An Aspect of Russian Mediaeval Political Theory', *Journal of the History of Ideas*, 4 (1959), pp. 459–76. For a balanced estimation of the influence of Mongolian political culture on Muscovy, see Charles Halperin, *The Tatar Yoke: The Image of the Mongols in Medieval Russia* (Bloomington, IN, 2009).
4 Richard Wortman explores in far greater detail the rituals of the monarchs from Peter's age onward: see R. Wortman, *Scenarios of Power: Myth and Ceremony in Russian Monarchy from Peter the Great to the Abdication of Nicholas II* (Princeton, NJ, 2006).
5 An excellent rebuke of those who believe Russians are 'born to slavery' is Nancy Shields Kollmann, *Kinship and Politics: The Making of the Muscovite Political System, 1345–1547* (Stanford, CA, 1987); regarding the idea that Russians are servile by nature, see M. Poe, *'A People Born to Slavery': Russia in Early Modern European Ethnography, 1476–1748* (Ithaca, NY, 2001).
6 Among his numerous works, see N. Berdyaev, *The Russian Idea* (New York, 1948), and N. Berdyaev, *The Origin of Russian Communism* (New York, 1937).

7 See, among many others, B. Anderson, *Imagined Communities*, revd edn (London, 2006); E. Hobsbawm and T. Ranger, eds, *The Invention of Tradition* (Cambridge, 1983). See also G. Carleton, *Russia: The Story of War* (Cambridge, MA, 2017). Carleton is undoubtedly correct in arguing for an intertwining of Russians' identity with martial prowess (or suffering to the bitter end) in war in the propaganda served up by Kremlin ideologues and other nationalist demagogues, but how much traction this myth has among the (often utterly cynical) Russian population is hard to measure. A sort of military pride informs most nationalist myths: thus, the Turks say that 'every Turk is born a soldier,' an expression rooted in the Turkish (Kemalist) and Ottoman past, which was as much or even more characterized by warfare as Russian history. In both countries, universal male conscription exists: undoubtedly, this infuses the minds of young men with ideas regarding duty and obedience to their mother- or fatherland.

8 The full title that he took was 'Great Sovereign, by God's grace Tsar and Grand Prince of all Rus', Vladimir, Moscow, Novgorod, Pskov, Ryazan, Tver', Jugurthia, Perm, Viatka, Bolgariia and others'.

9 I tend to agree with Marshall Poe that, because of its history and geography and despite many similarities with other cultures or civilizations, Russia is neither truly part of Europe nor of Asia, but in a sense a separate continent: see M. Poe, *The Russian Moment in World History* (Princeton, NJ, 2003). Without the Middle-Asian and Transcaucasian republics, Russia's geographic position in Eurasia is not unlike that of the southern subcontinent of India, Pakistan, Nepal, Bhutan, Sikkim and Bangladesh, or indeed like Europe west of the Dniestr and Bug rivers (more or less looking westward from the current Polish-Ukrainian and Polish-Belarusian borders). Still, these western borders, even if fixed since 1945, are hardly precise. It may be apt that Ukraine means 'borderland', for it is difficult to say where the Eastern Slavic world ends and 'Europe' begins. It is similarly difficult to pinpoint the exact border between the Russian world and Central Asia, not least because a country such as Kazakhstan still has some 40 per cent Slavic inhabitants (like, by the way, Latvia).

10 For more, see especially Charles Halperin, *Russia and the Golden Horde: The Mongol Impact on Medieval Russian History* (Bloomington, IN, 1987). See as well David Morgan, *The Mongols*, 2nd edn (Oxford, 2007).
11 As Tver' found out in 1327, the Mongols met rebellion with harsh retribution.
12 Kliuchevskii's work is still only in part translated into English. His discussion (part of his course on Russian history) can be found in V. O. Kliuchevskii, *Sochineniia* (Moscow, 1956), pp. 292–315.
13 Excellent on this is Mikhail Khodarkovsky, *Russia's Steppe Frontier: The Making of a Colonial Empire, 1500–1800* (Bloomington, IN, 2002). For a more general treatment, see Andreas Kappeler, *The Russian Empire: A Multi-ethnic History* (London, 2001).
14 Ruslan Khasbulatov (b. 1942), the speaker of Boris Yeltsin's first Russian parliament, is an ethnic Chechen, as is Vladislav Surkov, long-serving chief of the Russian presidential administration (b. 1964); Sergei Shoigu (b. 1955), the longest serving minister in the post-Soviet government, is half-Tuva; Sergei Lavrov (b. 1950), the foreign minister, is half-Armenian, and so on.
15 See, for example, H. G. Koenigsberger, 'Monarchies and Parliaments in Early Modern Europe', *Theory and Society*, v/2 (1978), pp. 191–217; J. H. Elliott, 'A Europe of Composite Monarchies', *Past and Present*, 137 (1992), pp. 48–71.
16 M. P. Romaniello, *The Elusive Empire: Kazan and the Creation of Russia, 1552–1671* (Madison, WI, 2012).
17 See Richard Hellie, ed., *The Muscovite Law Code (Ulozhenie) of 1649* (Irvine, CA, 1988).
18 See Khodarkovsky, *Russia's Steppe Frontier*, pp. 51–6.
19 The best two accounts of its birth and early years are R. Pipes, *The Formation of the Soviet Union: Communism and Nationalism, 1917–1923*, revd edn (Cambridge, MA, 1997); and Terry Martin, *The Affirmative Action Empire: Nations and Nationalism in the Soviet Union, 1923–1939* (Ithaca, NY, 2001).
20 Lowell Tillett, *The Great Friendship: Soviet Historians on the Non-Russian Nationalities* (Chapel Hill, NC, 1969).

21 For the distinction between soft- and hard-line Soviet policies, see Martin, *The Affirmative Action Empire*.
22 In 2010, slightly more than four-fifths of the population of 142 million of the Russian Federation was identified as ethnically Russian, while more than 160 other ethnic groups were counted in the census of that year. Apart from Tatars, Ukrainians, Bashkirs, Chuvash, Chechens and Armenians, all numbering more than 1 million people in Russia, almost 6 million non-Russian people lived in Russia as temporary workers, refugees or permanent residents. It should be noted that many culturally Russian people (by which I mean people whose first language is Russian) live outside of Russia, as in Latvia, Kazakhstan, Moldova, Belarus, Estonia and Ukraine (even if Crimea and eastern Ukraine are not considered Ukrainian but Russian, as the Russian government is inclined to do).
23 See Wilhelm Reich, *The Mass Psychology of Fascism*, 3rd edn (New York, 1970), for an interesting take. Carleton rightfully notices that such things are myths, figments of the imagination, but that they can take a powerful hold over people's minds (see Carleton, *Russia*). How far people truly are willing to sacrifice themselves at the altar of their country is impossible to tell. The 27 million Soviet deaths in the Second World War remain a world record, of course, but how many sacrificed themselves willingly is hard to know. More civilians than people in uniform or partisans were slaughtered by the Nazis; they did not necessarily choose to die for their country.
24 For an almost all-encompassing approach studying the European empires in comparison, see S. Berger and A. Miller, eds, *Nationalizing Empires* (Budapest and New York, 2015). Only essays on the Dutch and Belgians are missing in this collection.
25 It all leads one to a scene in Stanislav Govorukhin's 1990 documentary film *We Should Not Live Like This (Tak zhit' nel'zia)*, in which someone wonders why in such a big country as the Soviet Union people live so poorly, whereas in a small country such as the Netherlands everyone lives so well. Perhaps the Dutch had been wise in relinquishing Indonesia in 1949.

2 Empire by Design or Accident of History?

1 See Brian Boeck, 'When Peter I Was Forced to Settle for Less: Coerced Labor and Resistance in a Failed Russian Colony, 1695–1711', *Journal of Modern History*, III (2008), pp. 485–514.
2 R. Pipes, *Russia under the Old Regime*, 2nd edn (London, 1997).
3 Arnold J. Toynbee, *Civilization on Trial* (Oxford, 1948), pp. 164–83.
4 That Ukraine might have formed a sort of equal partnership with Russia similar to the Scottish-English United Kingdom has hardly ever been considered.
5 See Lewis H. Siegelbaum, *Stakhanovism and the Politics of Productivity in the USSR, 1935–1941* (Cambridge, 1990).
6 Perhaps most articulate remained Lenin's writing on this, but his work pre-dated the communist takeover (V. I. Lenin, 'The State and Revolution: The Marxist Theory of the State and the Tasks of the Proletariat in the Revolution', www.marxists.org, accessed 16 August 2019).
7 Whether or not apocryphal, it seems apt that in the October 1917 days Lenin is supposed to have said '*on s'engage et puis on voit*' ('one gets involved and then just sees what happens'), a phrase attributed to Napoléon Bonaparte when he took over in France in 1799.
8 The name *Bolshevik* means 'those of the majority', which Lenin's followers acquired before the 1917 revolution when they gained majority support during a rather arcane conflict between several factions within the Russian Social Democratic party.

3 The Russian Empire in Western Eyes

1 His most famous novel is V. Maximov, *The Seven Days of Creation* (New York, 1975).
2 See J. V. Stalin, 'Speech to Business Executives', www.marxists.org, 4 February 1931 ('industrial managers' perhaps is a more apt translation than 'business executives').
3 For recently published works that carry this tone, see T. Snyder, *The Road to Unfreedom: Russia, Europe, America* (New York, 2018); and Masha Gessen, *The Man without a Face: The Unlikely*

Rise of Vladimir Putin (New York, 2012). Whereas I do believe that it behooves everyone to be quite distrustful of Putin and his cronies, I am not sure that he is (smart enough to be) some sort of evil incarnate.

4 John LeDonne, *The Grand Strategy of the Russian Empire* (Oxford, 2004). On the concept in general, John Lewis Gaddis, *On Grand Strategy* (New York, 2018), is stimulating.

5 Henry Kamen, *Empire: How Spain Became a World Power, 1492–1763* (New York, 2003).

6 The 1633 death of his bellicose father, the Patriarch Filaret, aided his cause in this regard. Had Filaret lived, the war might have continued.

7 *Boyar*s is the generic name given to the highest nobles at the tsar's court.

8 Best work on this is Brian L. Davies, *Warfare, State and Society on the Black Sea Steppe, 1500–1700* (London, 2007).

9 M. Poe, '*A People Born to Slavery': Russia in Early Modern European Ethnography, 1476–1748* (Ithaca, NY, 2001); L. Wolff, *Inventing Eastern Europe: The Map of Civilization on the Mind of the Enlightenment* (Stanford, CA, 1994).

10 Lloyd Berry and Robert Crummey, *Rude and Barbarous Kingdom: Russia in the Accounts of Sixteenth-century English Voyagers* (Madison, WI, 1968). One is led to ponder how far the Western depiction of Russians as savages was eventually adopted by the Russian monarchs themselves, when Catherine the Great seemed to have nothing more than utter contempt for Russian culture, believing that her subjects were children who needed to get an education. This sort of disdainful attitude is also palpable in the behaviour of Catherine's grandson Nicholas I as tsar.

4 Prehistory and Geography: Rus'

1 Comte Robert de Montesquieu, *The Spirit of Laws*, book 14, chap. 2, https://oll.libertyfund.org, 8 January 2020.

2 A debate is still raging among historians as to when the first or proto-Slavs are mentioned; some believe they are to be equated with the (Vistula) Veneti mentioned by Tacitus (56–120) in 98 CE. Jordanes (*fl.* 550), half a millennium later, used the same name

for an ethnocultural group that may with greater certainty be identified as Slavonic.
3 For an overview of climate change in northern Europe, see Jan Esper et al., 'Orbital Forcing of Tree-ring Data', *Nature Climate Change*, II (2012), pp. 862–6.
4 A very good overview on all of this remains William H. McNeill, *Europe's Steppe Frontier* (Chicago, IL, 1964).
5 See S. H. Cross and O. P. Sherbowitz-Wetsor, eds, *The Russian Primary Chronicle, Laurentian Text* (Cambridge, MA, 1930), p. 59.
6 See Peter B. Golden et al., eds, *The World of the Khazars: New Perspectives* (Leiden, 2007).
7 Among the more important were Volyn (Volhynia), Halych (Galicia), Pereiaslav, Chernihiv (Chernigov), Polatsk, Smolensk, Novgorod, Pskov and Rostov-Vladimir-Suzdal'.
8 A phrase coined by the German historian Leopold von Ranke (1785–1886) that means '[to render the past] how it truly was'.

5 The Mongols, Siberia and Asia

1 See William H. McNeill, *Europe's Steppe Frontier* (Chicago, IL, 1964).
2 Depending on the language, in some sources they are called Qipchaks (a name also given to the Polovtsy before them), and in others Jochi.
3 Until very recently, motor vehicles, including lorries, were less significant because the construction of a sustainable network of highways proved prohibitively expensive. Although in recent years an asphalt road between European Russia and Vladivostok on the Pacific has been completed, it remains to be seen if such a lengthy highway can be maintained without incurring unreasonable cost.

6 Moscow's Rise: The Impact of the Byzantine, Polish-Lithuanian and Mongolian Empires on Muscovy

1 A most interesting case of a Russian merchant who spent many years away from his native land and moved from Orthodoxy to

Islam is Afanasii Nikitin (d. 1472), who left a truncated account of his travels that seems to attest to his gradual conversion.
2 *Mongolo-Tatarskoe Igo*, meaning 'Mongol Yoke', was a term coined by Polish writers around 1500.
3 Serhii Plokhy, *The Origins of the Slavic Nations: Premodern Identities in Russia, Ukraine, and Belarus* (Cambridge, 2006), p. 200.
4 See E. Weber, *Peasants into Frenchmen: The Modernization of Rural France, 1870–1914* (Stanford, CA, 1976).
5 S. von Herberstein, *Notes upon Russia*, trans. and ed. R. H. Major (London, 1851), p. 37.
6 The very first person who mentions this concept in writing was an ultimately disgraced metropolitan of Moscow, Zosima, in 1492 (in part because he read great significance in the Orthodox calendar: the Western calendar's 1492 was its year 7000).
7 G. Fletcher, *Of the Russe Commonwealth* [1591], ed. Richard Pipes (Cambridge, MA, 1966).

7 Troubles

1 As has been argued particularly for an earlier period, see Nancy Shields Kollmann, *Kinship and Politics: The Making of the Muscovite Political System, 1345–1547* (Stanford, CA, 1987).

8 From Mikhail to Peter: Composite Empire and Middle Ground

1 In addition to which later calamities (fires, as in 1812) and repeated reorganizations of the bureaucracy have caused many documents to disappear.
2 Most illuminating in describing this process are R. Hellie, *Enserfment and Military Change in Muscovy* (Chicago, IL, 1971); Carol Belkin Stevens, *Russia's Wars of Emergence, 1460–1730* (New York, 2007); Brian Davies, *State Power and Community in Early Modern Russia* (Basingstoke, 1994); Brian Davies, *Warfare, State and Society on the Black Sea Steppe, 1500–1700* (London, 2007).
3 Jarmo Kotilaine, 'When the Twain Did Meet: Foreign Merchants and Russia's Economic Expansion in the Seventeenth Century', PhD diss., Harvard University, 2000, pp. 36, 110–11.

4 G. Parker, *Global Crisis: War, Climate Change and Catastrophe in the Seventeenth Century* (New Haven, CT, 2013), p. 153.
5 M. P. Romaniello, *The Elusive Empire: Kazan and the Creation of Russia, 1552–1671* (Madison, WI, 2012); Mikhail Khodarkovsky, *Russia's Steppe Frontier: The Making of a Colonial Empire, 1500–1800* (Bloomington, IN, 2002).
6 Richard White, *The Middle Ground: Indians, Empires, and Republics in the Great Lakes Region, 1650–1815* (Cambridge, 1991).
7 R. Matthee, 'Relations between the Center and the Periphery in Safavid Iran: The Western Borderlands versus the Eastern Frontier Zone', *The Historian*, III (2015), pp. 431–63.
8 See L. Bernard, 'French Society and Popular Uprisings under Louis XIV, *French Historical Studies*, IV (1964), pp. 454–74.
9 And thus it is questionable whether or not the Time of Troubles was a true watershed, separating distinct periods within Muscovy's history.
10 Sometimes they are called 'Schismatics', or *Raskolniki*, used by Dostoyevsky for the protagonist of *Crime and Punishment*, Raskolnikov (see F. Dostoyevsky, *Crime and Punishment*, [London, 1982]).
11 And it should be remembered that the northern Black Sea littoral and Crimea remained under Tatar-Ottoman rule.
12 See K. Boterbloem, *The Fiction and Reality of Jan Struys: A Seventeenth-century Dutch Globetrotter* (Basingstoke, 2008).

9 The Waning of the Middle Ground: The Russian, French and British Empires, 1721–1853

1 See R. Pipes, *Russia under the Old Regime*, 2nd edn (London, 1997).
2 This affectation was criticized long before it was lampooned by Tolstoy in *War and Peace*: see Leo Tolstoy, *War and Peace*, (London, 1978).
3 See S. Usitalo, *The Invention of Mikhail Lomonosov: A Russian National Myth* (New York, 2013).
4 See R. Pipes, *Karamzin's Memoir on Ancient and Modern Russia*, 2nd edn (Ann Arbor, MI, 2005).

5. The Ottoman Turks patronized all Sunni Muslims because their sultan claimed at the same time to be the caliph, the religious chief of all (Sunni) Muslims.
6. The best work on 1812 is D. Lieven, *Russia against Napoleon: The True Story of the Campaigns of War and Peace* (New York, 2010).
7. See for example Henry Kissinger, *A World Restored: Metternich, Castlereagh and the Problems of Peace* (Boston, MA, 1957).
8. The rumour persists until this very day that Alexander absconded to Siberia, where he lived as the hermit Fyodor Kuzmich until the 1860s.
9. Paul Kennedy, *The Rise and Fall of the Great Powers: Economic Change and Military Conflict from 1500 to 2000* (New York, 1987).
10. Formally, because Grudzinska was of low noble birth and the marriage was therefore considered morganatic, her social status excluded Konstantin from the succession. This was odd, as Peter the Great's second wife Catherine had been a commoner, which had not stopped her from succeeding her husband in 1725. In effect, Konstantin, a rather unambitious fellow, seems to have declined his claim to the throne in the teeth of substantial opposition that he would have faced not merely because of Grudzinska's low birth but also because of her religion.

10 Indirect and Direct Rule: The Russian and British Empires in Asia, 1853–1907

1. See J. A. Hobson, *Imperialism: A Study* [1902], at www.marxists.org, accessed 6 August 2019.
2. See Bruno Naarden, 'Marx and Russia', *History of European Ideas*, VI (1990), pp. 783–97. On the loaded term 'oriental despotism' made popular by Wittfogel, see Perry Anderson, *Lineages of the Absolutist State* (New York, 1979); and Karl Wittfogel, *Oriental Despotism: A Comparative Study of Total Power* (New Haven, CT, 1957).
3. Andreas Kappeler, *The Russian Empire: A Multi-ethnic History* (London, 2001), pp. 263, 267.

References

11 Multinational Empires: Russia and Austria-Hungary, 1853–1917

1 For the census of 1897, see *demoskop weekly*, www.demoscope.ru, 27 November 2019.
2 M. Hroch, *Social Preconditions of National Revival in Europe* (Cambridge, 1985); and M. Hroch, *European Nations: Explaining their Formation* (London, 2015).
3 This is peculiar as the Socialist-Revolutionary main platform focused on the redistribution of all land among those who actually worked it, and should have appealed more than anything to the Slavic peasantry. Jews were largely forbidden to own land in the Russian empire.
4 See O. Bauer, *Die Nationalitätenfrage und die Sozialdemokratie* (Vienna, 1907).
5 For its full text in English, see [K. Stalin], 'Marxism and the Nationality Question', www.marxists.org, accessed 9 January 2020.
6 See Paul R. Gregory, *Before Command: An Economic History Of Russia from Emancipation to the First Five Year Plan* (Princeton, NJ, 1994); Philip Longworth, *The Making of Eastern Europe* (Basingstoke, 1992), p. 111.

12 The Soviet Union as Empire, 1917–91

1 Apart from Austria (-Hungary), which inherited the imperial title from the defunct Holy Roman Empire (dissolved by Napoléon), Germany also called itself a *Kaiserreich*, after its unification in 1870. The Ottoman sultan in Istanbul claimed to be the successor to the Byzantine emperors.
2 In linking Soviet and Russian history, Arnold Toynbee aptly quoted an aphorism by the Roman author Horace, 'You may throw Nature out with a pitchfork, but she will keep coming back' (Arnold J. Toynbee, *Civilization on Trial* [Oxford, 1948], p.164). The Soviets introduced a new calendar, a ten-day week and other things similar to the iconoclastic new months and years introduced by the French revolutionaries during the 1790s, but as with the undeniable French essence of those revolutionaries, the

quintessential Russian quality of the Communists could not quite be exorcized.

3 In a rather confusing fashion, soon after the October 1917 coup the leadership of the new, Communist, Russia began to be called Soviet, both at home and abroad; the word literally means 'council' in Russian, and referred in the 1917 revolution to the meetings of workers', sailors', and soldiers' representatives in the main cities that gathered to express approval or denounce decisions made by the caretaker (provisional) government that succeeded the tsar's administration. Lenin suggested that these soviets embodied the real voice of the people and should take power themselves; in their name, then, Lenin proceeded to take power in October 1917, using some sophistry to suggest that his Council of People's Commissars was the government backed by all the country's soviets. Subsequently, the name Soviet became synonymous with the Communist regime, especially when various soviet republics (as well as the Union of Socialist Soviet Republics) were officially founded in subsequent years.

4 Time reckoning is Old (Julian) Style here; in early 1918 the Soviets adopted the Western (Gregorian) calendar.

5 'Empire' may not be the right word, as this was to be a society of enlightened equal and free individuals, which would not need any real government, according to both Marx and Lenin.

6 Those republics were those of the Russian Socialist Federative Soviet Republic (RSFSR), the Ukrainian Socialist Soviet Republic [UKSSR], the Belorussian SSR, and the Transcaucasian SSR. In 1925, the Turkmen and Uzbek SSRs were added (of which the Tajik SSR was split off in 1929). The Kazakh and Kirghiz SSRs, after they had been autonomous republics of the RSFSR, were only formed in 1936, when the 'Stalin Constitution' was adopted. At the same time the Transcaucasian SSR split into the Armenian, Azeri and Georgian SSRs. After the 1939 Molotov-Ribbentrop Pact allowed Soviet Russia a free hand in the Baltic region, the Estonian, Latvian and Lithuanian SSRs appeared in 1940 (and were reconstituted at the end of the Second World War in 1945). The last of the fifteen republics that formed the Soviet Union in the post-war era was the Moldavian SSR, which occupied more or less the territory of the former tsarist Bessarabia, and was first

founded in 1940, when a significant part of Romanian Moldavia was annexed (again more or less on the basis of the Nazi-Soviet agreement of August 1939), and then re-established in 1944, when it was wholly occupied by Soviet forces.

7 R. Pipes, *The Formation of the Soviet Union: Communism and Nationalism, 1917–1923*, revd edn (Cambridge, MA, 1997); Terry Martin, *The Affirmative Action Empire: Nations and Nationalism in the Soviet Union, 1923–1939* (Ithaca, NY, 2001).

8 Indeed, throughout the entire Soviet Union perhaps more than half of the population was able to send their children to any school for the first time ever in history.

9 The best book on this remains Michael Voslensky, *Nomenklatura: The Soviet Ruling Class* (New York, 1984). Enlightening as well is Georgy Arbatov, *The System: An Insider's Life in Soviet Politics* (New York, 1992).

10 See V. I. Lenin, 'Imperialism, the Highest State of Capitalism', www.marxists.org, accessed 10 January 2020.

11 See Lowell Tillett, *The Great Friendship: Soviet Historians on the Non-Russian Nationalities* (Chapel Hill, NC, 1969).

12 Although they quarrelled about this towards the end of Lenin's life, Lenin and Stalin implicitly appear to have agreed that their country would use Russian as its lingua franca.

13 *Gulag* stands for *Glavnoe Upravlenie Lagerei*, the 'main administration of camps', the NKVD department which oversaw the Soviet concentration camps. (NKVD stands for *Narodnyi komissariat vnutrennykh del*, or People's Commissariat of Internal Affairs). The term *Gulag Archipelago* was invented by the former camp inmate Aleksandr Solzhenitsyn; see his three-part oral history published in the original Russian in Paris from 1973 to 1975: A. Solzhenitsyn, *Arkhipelag GULAG: Opyt khudozhestvennogo issledovaniia, 1918–1956* (Paris, 1973–5), in English: A. Solzhenitsyn, *The Gulag Archipelago*, 3 vols (New York, 1973–8). In placing the staggering number of Stalinist concentration camps on a map, Solzhenitsyn realized that they resembled islands within a sea of territory populated by 'free' Soviet citizens.

14 Some of his thoughts after his 1957 retirement were recorded in conversations with a Soviet journalist; their most salient

exchanges can be perused in English in F. Chuev, *Molotov Remembers: Inside Kremlin Politics* (Chicago, IL, 1993).
15 The scholarship in Russian is quite good, but the topic deserves more study in English.
16 The Iranian Shah Abbas the Great had most of his Armenian and Georgian subjects relocate from their homeland in the Caucasus region to his capital of Isfahan in the early seventeenth century. The two key works on Stalin's deportations are A. M. Nekrich, *The Punished Peoples* (New York, 1981); and P. Polyan, *Against Their Will: The History and Geography of Forced Migrations in the USSR* (Budapest, 2003).
17 'Ethnic cleansing' was a term that seems to have been introduced around this time by the German chief Heinrich Himmler for this sort of policy. An excellent overview may be found in T. Snyder, *Bloodlands: Europe between Hitler and Stalin* (London, 2010).
18 See G. Gorodetsky, *Grand Delusion: Stalin and the German Invasion of Russia* (New Haven, CT, 1999), and, for a brief summary, K. Boterbloem, *A History of Russia and Its Empire*, 2nd edn (Lanham, MD, 2018), pp. 230–36.
19 According to numbers provided by the World Bank (www.worldbank.org, 28 November 2019). Ukraine's per capita income is only 20 per cent higher than India's.

13 Since 1991: *Russkii* or *Rossiiskii*?

1 For a rather radical take on the effect of empire on the Russian mindset, see Alexander Etkind, *Internal Colonization: Russia's Imperial Experience* (Cambridge, 2011). Etkind's insights are thought-provoking, but say little about the actual course of imperial expansion. See, too, Gerard Toal, *Near Abroad: Putin, the West and the Contest over Ukraine and the Caucasus* (Oxford, 2017).
2 This happened especially in Uzbekistan and Kyrgyzstan, while the Russian and Ukrainian minority in Moldova entrenched themselves in Transnistria, defended by a part of the former Soviet army.
3 See Thomas de Waal, *Black Garden: Armenia and Azerbaijan through Peace and War*, revd edn (New York, 2013).

4 See Mark Galeotti, *Russia's Wars in Chechnya, 1994–2009* (Oxford, 2014).
5 H. Kuromiya, *Freedom and Terror in the Donbas: A Ukrainian-Russian Borderland* (Cambridge, 1998).
6 An interesting contemplation on the relationship between Russians and non-Russians in the Arctic is Yuri Slezkine, *Arctic Mirrors* (Ithaca, NY, 1994).

Afterword: Is the Age of Political Empires Over?

1 See Anthony Marx, *Faith in Nation: Exclusionary Origins of Nationalism* (Oxford, 2003).
2 V. I. Lenin, 'Imperialism, the Highest State of Capitalism', www.marxists.org, accessed 10 January 2020.

Bibliography

Anderson, Benedict, *Imagined Communities*, revd edn (London, 2006)
Anderson, Perry, *Lineages of the Absolutist State* (New York, 1979)
Arbatov, Georgy, *The System: An Insider's Life in Soviet Politics* (New York, 1992)
Barrett, Thomas, *At the Edge of Empire: The Terek Cossacks and the North Caucasus Frontier, 1700–1860* (Boulder, CO, 1999)
Bauer, Otto, *Die Nationalitätenfrage und die Sozialdemokratie* (Vienna, 1907)
Berdyaev, N., *The Origin of Russian Communism* (New York, 1937)
—, *The Russian Idea* (New York, 1948)
Berger, S., and A. Miller, eds, *Nationalizing Empires* (Budapest and New York, 2015)
Bernard, L., 'French Society and Popular Uprisings under Louis XIV', *French Historical Studies*, III/4 (1964), pp. 454–74
Berry, Lloyd, and Robert Crummey, *Rude and Barbarous Kingdom: Russia in the Accounts of Sixteenth-century English Voyagers* (Madison, WI, 1968)
Billington, James, *The Icon and the Axe: An Interpretive History of Russian Culture* (New York, 1966)
Boeck, Brian, 'When Peter I Was Forced to Settle for Less: Coerced Labor and Resistance in a Failed Russian Colony, 1695–1711', *Journal of Modern History*, LXXX/3 (2008), pp. 485–514
Boterbloem, Kees, *The Fiction and Reality of Jan Struys: A Seventeenth-century Dutch Globetrotter* (Basingstoke, 2008)
—, *A History of Russia and Its Empire: From Mikhail Romanov to Vladimir Putin*, 2nd edn (Lanham, MD, 2018)
Bushkovitch, Paul, *A Concise History of Russia* (Cambridge, 2011)

Carleton, G., *Russia: The Story of War* (Cambridge, MA, 2017)
[Census of 1897], *demoskop weekly*, www.demoscope.ru, 27 November 2019
Cherniavsky, Mikhail, '*Khan* or *Basileus*: An Aspect of Russian Mediaeval Political Theory', *Journal of the History of Ideas*, XX/4 (1959), pp. 459–76
Chew, Allen F., *An Atlas of Russian History: Eleven Centuries of Changing Borders* (New Haven, CT, 1967)
Chuev, F., *Molotov Remembers: Inside Kremlin Politics* (Chicago, IL, 1993)
Davies, Brian, *State Power and Community in Early Modern Russia* (Basingstoke, 1994)
—, *Warfare, State and Society on the Black Sea Steppe* (London, 2007)
Davies, Norman, *Europe: A History* (Oxford, 1996)
Dostoyevsky, F., *Crime and Punishment* (London, 1982)
Dunning, Chester, *Russia's First Civil War: The Time of Troubles and the Founding of the Romanov Dynasty* (University Park, PA, 2001)
Elias, Norbert, *The Civilizing Process: Sociogenetic and Psychogenetic Investigations*, revd edn (Oxford, 2000)
Elliott, J. H., 'A Europe of Composite Monarchies', *Past and Present*, CXXXVII/1 (1992), pp. 48–71
Esper, Jan, et al., 'Orbital Forcing of Tree-ring Data', *Nature Climate Change*, II/12 (2012), pp. 862–6
Etkind, Alexander, *Internal Colonization: Russia's Imperial Experience* (Cambridge, 2011)
Fletcher, Giles, *Of the Russe Commonwealth*, ed. Richard Pipes (Cambridge, MA, 1966)
Forsyth, James, *A History of the Peoples of Siberia: Russia's North Asian Colony, 1581–1990* (Cambridge, 1991)
Foucault, Michel, *The Order of Things: Introduction to the Archeology of Human Sciences* (New York, 1970)
Gaddis, John Lewis, *On Grand Strategy* (New York, 2018)
Galeotti, Mark, *Russia's Wars in Chechnya, 1994–2009* (Oxford, 2014)
Gessen, Masha, *The Man without a Face: The Unlikely Rise of Vladimir Putin* (New York, 2012)
Golden., Peter B., et al., eds, *The World of the Khazars: New Perspectives* (Leiden, 2007)

Goldfrank, D., L. Hughes, C. Evtuhov and R. Stites, *A History of Russia: Peoples, Legends, Events, Forces* (Boston, MA, 2004)

Gorodetsky, G., *Grand Delusion: Stalin and the German Invasion of Russia* (New Haven, CT, 1999)

Gregory, Paul R., *Before Command: An Economic History of Russia from Emancipation to the First Five Year Plan* (Princeton, NJ, 1994)

Halperin, Charles, *Russia and the Golden Horde: The Mongol Impact on Medieval Russian History* (Bloomington, IN, 1987)

—, *The Tatar Yoke: The Image of the Mongols in Medieval Russia* (Bloomington, IN, 2009)

Hellie, R., *Enserfment and Military Change in Muscovy* (Chicago, IL, 1971)

Herberstein, S. von, *Notes upon Russia*, trans. and ed. R. H. Major (London, 1851)

Hobsbawm, E., *The Age of Empire, 1875–1914* (New York, 1989)

—, and T. Ranger, *The Invention of Tradition* (Cambridge, 1983)

Hobson, J. A., *Imperialism: A Study*, at www.marxists.org, accessed 8 January 2020

Hosking, Geoffrey, *Russia: People and Empire* (Cambridge, MA, 1997)

—, *Russia and the Russians: A History* (Cambridge, MA, 2001)

Hroch, M., *European Nations: Explaining their Formation* (London, 2015)

—, *Social Preconditions of National Revival in Europe* (Cambridge, 1985)

Kamen, Henry, *Empire: How Spain Became a World Power, 1492–1763* (New York, 2003)

Kappeler, Andreas, *The Russian Empire: A Multi-ethnic History* (London, 2001)

Kennedy, Paul, *The Rise and Fall of the Great Powers: Economic Change and Military Conflict from 1500 to 2000* (New York, 1987)

Khalid, Adeeb, *Making Uzbekistan: Nation, Empire and Revolution in the Early USSR* (Ithaca, NY, 2015)

Khlevniuk, Oleg, *Stalin: New Biography of a Dictator* (New Haven, CT, 2015)

Khodarkovsky, Mikhail, *Russia's Steppe Frontier: The Making of a Colonial Empire, 1500–1800* (Bloomington, IN, 2002)

Kissinger, Henry, *A World Restored: Metternich, Castlereagh and the Problems of Peace* (Boston, MA, 1957)

Kivelson, V. A., and R. G. Suny, *Russia's Empires* (Oxford, 2016)
Kliuchevskii, V. O., *Sochineniia* (Moscow, 1956)
Koenigsberger, H. G., 'Monarchies and Parliaments in Early Modern Europe', *Theory and Society*, v/2 (1978), pp. 191–217
Kollmann, Nancy Shields, *Kinship and Politics: The Making of the Muscovite Political System, 1345–1547* (Stanford, CA, 1987)
Kotilaine, Jarmo, 'When the Twain Did Meet: Foreign Merchants and Russia's Economic Expansion in the Seventeenth Century', PhD diss., Harvard University, 2000
Kotkin, Stephen, *Stalin*, 2 vols (New York, 2015–17)
Kumar, Krishan, *Visions of Empire: How Five Imperial Regimes Shaped the World* (Princeton, NJ, 2017)
Kuromiya, H., *Freedom and Terror in the Donbas: A Ukrainian-Russian Borderland* (Cambridge, 1998)
LeDonne, John, *The Grand Strategy of the Russian Empire* (Oxford, 2004)
Lenin, V. I., 'Imperialism, the Highest State of Capitalism' [1917], www.marxists.org, accessed 8 January 2020
—, 'The State and Revolution: The Marxist Theory of the State and the Tasks of the Proletariat in the Revolution' [1917], www.marxists.org, accessed 8 January 2020
Lieven, D., *Russia against Napoleon: The True Story of the Campaigns of War and Peace* (New York, 2010)
Longworth, Philip, *The Making of Eastern Europe* (Basingstoke, 1992)
—, *Russia: The Once and Future Empire from Pre-history to Putin* (New York, 2005)
McNeill, William H., *Europe's Steppe Frontier* (Chicago, IL, 1964)
Magosci, Paul Robert, *Historical Atlas of East Central Europe* (Toronto, 1993)
Martin, Terry, *The Affirmative Action Empire: Nations and Nationalism in the Soviet Union, 1923–1939* (Ithaca, NY, 2001)
Marx, Anthony, *Faith in Nation: Exclusionary Origins of Nationalism* (Oxford, 2003)
Matthee, R., 'Was Safavid Iran an Empire?', *Journal of the Economic and Social History of the Orient*, LIII/1–2 (2010), pp. 233–65
—, 'Relations between the Center and the Periphery in Safavid Iran: The Western Borderlands versus the Eastern Frontier Zone', *The Historian*, LXVII/3 (2015), pp. 431–63
Maximov, V., *The Seven Days of Creation* (New York, 1975)

Montesquieu, Comte Robert de, *The Spirit of the Laws* (New York, 1949)
Morgan, David, *The Mongols*, 2nd edn (Oxford, 2007)
Moss, Walter G., *A History of Russia*, 2 vols, 2nd edn (London, 2005)
The Muscovite Law Code (Ulozhenie) of 1649, ed. Richard Hellie (Irvine, CA, 1988)
Naarden, Bruno, 'Marx and Russia', *History of European Ideas*, XII/6 (1990), pp. 783–97
Nekrich, A. M., *The Punished Peoples* (New York, 1981)
Ostrowski, Donald, *Muscovy and the Mongols: Cross-cultural Influences on the Steppe Frontier, 1304–1589* (Cambridge, 1998)
Parker, G., *Global Crisis: War, Climate Change and Catastrophe in the Seventeenth Century* (New Haven, CT, 2013)
Pipes, R., *The Formation of the Soviet Union: Communism and Nationalism, 1917–1923*, revd edn (Cambridge, MA, 1997)
—, *Karamzin's Memoir on Ancient and Modern Russia*, 2nd edn (Ann Arbor, MI, 2005)
—, *Russia under the Old Regime*, 2nd edn (London, 1997)
Plokhy, Serhii, *The Origins of the Slavic Nations: Premodern Identities in Russia, Ukraine, and Belarus* (Cambridge, 2006)
Poe, M., *'A People Born to Slavery': Russia in Early Modern European Ethnography, 1476–1748* (Ithaca, NY, 2001)
—, *The Russian Moment in World History* (Princeton, NJ, 2003)
Polyan, P., *Against Their Will: The History and Geography of Forced Migrations in the USSR* (Budapest, 2003)
Ree, Erik van, *The Political Thought of Joseph Stalin: A Study in Twentieth Century Revolutionary Patriotism* (London, 2003)
Reich, Wilhelm, *The Mass Psychology of Fascism*, 3rd edn (New York, 1970)
Riasanovsky, N., and Mark Steinberg, *A History of Russia*, 8th edn (Oxford, 2010)
Romaniello, M. P., *The Elusive Empire: Kazan and the Creation of Russia, 1552–1671* (Madison, WI, 2012)
The Russian Primary Chronicle, Laurentian Text, ed. S. H. Cross and O. P. Sherbowitz-Wetsor (Cambridge, MA, 1930)
Seton-Watson, Hugh, *The Russian Empire, 1801–1917* (Oxford, 1917)
Siegel, Jennifer, *Britain, Russia and the Final Struggle for Central Asia* (London, 2002)

Siegelbaum, Lewis H., *Stakhanovism and the Politics of Productivity in the USSR, 1935–1941* (Cambridge, 1990)
Slezkine, Yuri, *Arctic Mirrors* (Ithaca, NY, 1994)
—, *The Jewish Century*, new edn (New Haven, CT, 2019)
Snyder, T., *Bloodlands: Europe between Hitler and Stalin* (London, 2010)
—, *The Road to Unfreedom: Russia, Europe, America* (New York, 2018)
Solzhenitsyn, A., *Arkhipelag GULAG: Opyt khudozhestvennogo issledovaniia, 1918–1956*, 3 vols (Paris, 1973–5)
—, *The Gulag Archipelago*, 3 vols (New York, 1973–8)
Stevens, Carol Belkin, *Russia's Wars of Emergence, 1460–1730* (New York, 2007)
Subtelny, Orest, *Ukraine: A History*, 4th edn (Toronto, 2009)
Sunderland, Willard, *Taming the Wild Field: Colonization and Empire on the Russian Steppe* (Ithaca, NY, 2004)
Suny, Ronald Grigor, *Looking after Ararat: Armenia in Modern History* (Bloomington, IN, 1993)
—, *The Making of the Georgian Nation*, 2nd edn (Bloomington, IN, 1994)
Stalin, Josef, 'Speech to Business Executives', 4 February 1931, www.marxists.org
[Stalin, K], 'Marxism and the Nationality Question', www.marxists.org, accessed 27 November 2019
Tillett, Lowell, *The Great Friendship: Soviet Historians on the Non-Russian Nationalities* (Chapel Hill, NC, 1969)
Toal, Gerard, *Near Abroad: Putin, the West and the Contest over Ukraine and the Caucasus* (Oxford, 2017)
Tolstoy, Leo, *War and Peace* (London, 1978)
Toynbee, Arnold J., *Civilization on Trial* (Oxford, 1948)
Ulam, Adam B., *Expansion and Coexistence: Soviet Foreign Policy, 1917–1973*, 2nd edn (New York, 1974)
Usitalo, S., *The Invention of Mikhail Lomonosov: A Russian National Myth* (New York, 2013)
Voslensky, Michael, *Nomenklatura: The Soviet Ruling Class* (New York, 1984)
Waal, Thomas de, *Black Garden: Armenia and Azerbaijan through Peace and War*, revd edn (New York, 2013)
Weber, E., *Peasants into Frenchmen: The Modernization of Rural France, 1870–1914* (Stanford, CA, 1976)

Westad, Odd Arne, *The Cold War: A World History* (New York, 2017)
White, Hayden, 'Foucault Decoded: Notes from Underground', *History and Theory*, XII/1 (1973), pp. 23–54
White, Richard, *The Middle Ground: Indians, Empires, and Republics in the Great Lakes Region, 1650–1815* (Cambridge, 1991)
Wittfogel, Karl, *Oriental Despotism: A Comparative Study of Total Power* (New Haven, CT, 1957)
Wolff, L., *Inventing Eastern Europe: The Map of Civilization on the Mind of the Enlightenment* (Stanford, CA, 1994)
[WorldBank statistics] www.worldbank.org, 28 November 2019
Wortman, R., *Scenarios of Power: Myth and Ceremony in Russian Monarchy from Peter the Great to the Abdication of Nicholas II* (Princeton, NJ, 2006)
Zubok, V. M., *A Failed Empire: The Soviet Union in the Cold War from Stalin to Gorbachev*, 2nd edn (Chapel Hill, NC, 2007)
Zygar, Mikhail, *All the Kremlin's Men: Inside the Court of Vladimir Putin* (New York, 2016)

Acknowledgements

Ben Hayes, then with Reaktion Books, approached me several years ago to consider writing a book on Russia as an empire. By being eminently flexible with the timeline, Michael Leaman kept this project alive after I threatened to be buried under other publishing commitments. Amy Salter was essential in bringing this book to completion. All three therefore deserve my profound gratitude! Of course, I am thankful to everyone else at Reaktion Books who has worked on its production.

As usual, the number of scholars and thinkers whose words and advice inform this book is vast and it would take several pages to name them all. But several of those who fanned the flames of my passion for Russian and Soviet history deserve to be praised by name: W. H. Roobol, Marc Jansen, Jan-Willem Bezemer, Martin van den Heuvel, Valentin Boss and Philip Longworth, not least because their teaching and writing grappled with the phenomenon of the Russian empires. Erik van Ree has been a guiding light as a foremost expert on Stalin as a thinker, especially on the topic of nationalities in the Russian and Soviet empires. Charles Halperin's writing on the Mongols (and other things) deserves much credit for shaping my work in this regard, while on Ukraine the exceptionally fine scholarly works by Serhy Yekelchyk, Serhii Plokhy and Karel Berkhoff have set a standard. Hiroaki Kuromiya's work inspired for its similar even-handedness and scholarly brilliance. Equally inspiring have been Rudolf Dekker, Paul Robinson and Bruno Naarden. Rawil Fakhrullin has sharpened my thinking about ethnocultural communities in Russia in recent times. As always, my wife, Dr Susan Mooney, and my children, Duncan and Saskia Mooney, have aided in myriad ways in helping me complete this book (not least in tolerating a distracted and grumpy husband and father), for which I remain forever in their debt!

Photo Acknowledgements

The author and publishers wish to express their thanks to the below sources of illustrative material and/or permission to reproduce it.

Sebastian Ballard: pp. 18–19, 68–9, 102, 122, 142–3; Prokudin-Gorskiĭ Collection, Library of Congress, Prints and Photographs Division, Washington, DC: pp. 29, 73, 79, 80, 83, 93, 115, 145, 147, 148, 149, 150, 153, 154, 161, 163, 170, 171, 182.

Index

Page numbers in *italics* refer to illustrations

1905 Revolution 146, 162
1917 Revolution 9–11, 15, 24, 41–2, 75, 166–7, 169, 174–5

abolition of serfdom (1861) 32, 131, 140–41
absolutism 20, 92, 190; *see also* autocracy
Academy of Sciences 118–19
Afghanistan 14, 54, 76, 135, 146, 191, 193
Africa 38, 150–51, 154–5, 192
agriculture 41, 59, 65, 74, 131, 151, 177
Alaska 40, 74–5, 134
Alexander the Great 43, 48
Alexander I 130–33, 158
Alexander II 10, 32, 40, 140–41
Alexander III 34, 157, 159–60
Aleksei Mikhailovich 14, 31, 46, 49, 51–3, 82, 109–14, 166, 201
America 38, 46, 71, 74, 107, 121, 135
Anastasia Zakhar'ina-Iur'eva 89
Andropov, Yuri 192
Anna Ioannovna 39, 123, 129
antiquity 17, 20, 118
anti-Semitism 189

Aral Sea 149
Arctic 94
Arkhangel'sk 53, 88, 110, 114–15
Armenia 155, 170, *171*, 196
army (arms) 20–21, 29–33, 37, 39, 48–53, 56, 71–4, 84–5, 88–90, 94–9, 101, 103–19, 123–4, 129, 131–3, 137, 140–8, 151–5, 167–70, 174, 177–8, 180–83, 189–91, 197, 200–202, 205, 207
artisans 116
Assembly of the Land 94, 110
Astrakhan 51, 88, 113
ataman (supreme Cossack chief) 110, 138
atomic bomb 189
Augustus 119
Aurangzeb 107
Austria 15, 56, 130, 135–6, 152, 156, 158–9, 162–3, *163*, 166, 209
autocracy 21–2, 55, 92, 99–100, 125–7, 130, 137, 139, 160–62, 177
Avars 59, 62, 66
Azerbaijan 132, 151, 170, *171*, 196
Azov 22, 39, 52, 54, 109, 115–16

235

backwardness 125, 136, 140, 176
Baku 151
balkanization 195
Balkans 133
Baltic Germans 28, 82, 88–9, 155, 187
Baltic region (states) 39, 45, 53–4, 56, 79, 89, 109, 119, 131, 134, 156, 160, 166–9, 179, 183, 185, 196, 200–202, 207
Baltic Sea 40, 46, 49, 51, 61, 65, 79, 84, 108, 116
Bashkirs 34, 107, 121, 123
Basmachi rebellion 30, 170
battles (significant) 54–5, 58, 84, 117–18, 131, 133, 146, 188
beards 118
Beccaria, Cesare 126
Belarus(yns/sians) 12, 34–5, 37, 52, 59, 61–7, 79, 80–82, 95, 104, 125, 138, 156, 159, 169, 185–7
Belgium 25, 116, 133, 136
Bering, Vitus 74
Bismarck, Otto von 157, 162
Black Hundreds 161–2
Black Sea 40, 46, 55, 59, 62–3, 65, 84, 90, 116
Bolotnikov, Ivan 97
Bolsheviks 15, 42, 168
Boris Godunov 92, 94–6, 105
botik 113, *115*
Boxer revolt 144
boyars 52, 89, 92, 95–100, 106, 118, 125
Brezhnev, Leonid 9, 190–92
British alliance with Russia (1907) 146

Brius (Bruce), Iakov 129
Bukhara *153*
Bulavin, Fyodor 121
Bulgaria 20
bureaucracy 32, 99, 104–5, 121, 159, 173
Byzantine Empire 8, 12–13, 17, 20–21, 26–7, 40, 50, 61–2, 85–6, 120

caesar (*-opapism*) 9, 20, 25, 113, 119
canals 151
capitalism 168, 174, 199
Caspian Sea 39–40, 46, 51, 53–4, 62, 65–6, 72, 113, 123, 132, 151, *171*
Catherine II, the Great 11, 14, 31, 53, 55–6, 85, *122*, 124, 126–31, 137
Catholicism (Roman) 49, 52, 54, 78, 84, 87, 95–6, 138, 159–60
Catholics (Greek or Ukrainian) *see* Uniates
Caucasus 76, 82, 123–4, 150, 156, 160, *170*, 213
cavalry 66, 88, 101, 104
censorship 129, 137
censuses 62, 156–7, 162, 183–4
Central Asia 14, 29, 32–3, 40, 54, 72–3, *73*, 75–6, 123, *143*, 144–8, *148*, *150*, 150–53, *153*, 156, 160, 170, 186–7, 205
Central Committee 169, 173
Central Powers 166–8
Chaadaev, Pyotr 129
Chancery Slavonic 67, 80, 84

Charles v 47–9, 86
Charles XII 117–18
Chechens 34, 132, 183, 186, 195–6, 203, 207
Cherkess(ians) 28, 124, 132
Chernenko, Konstantin 192
Chernobyl 193
China 8, 25–6, 39–40, 47, 54–5, 70, 74, 76, 123, 135, 144–6, 149, 152, 170, 183, 189–92, 204–6
Chingis Khan 12, 15, 48
Chingisids 13, 43, 67, 70
Christianization 11, 67
chronicles 56, 61–3, 65
church bells 117
Church Slavonic 67
Churchill, Winston 187
civil war 14, 36, 165, 167–9, 181–2; *see also* Time of Troubles
civilization 32, 45, 124, 131, 150, 152, 208
clergy 28, 52, 62, 95–6, 98–9, 110–11, 162, 184
climate 13, 36, 59–60, 89, 92
codes (legal) 30–31, *see also* Ulozhenie
Cold War 45, 48, 146, 189, 202
collective farming 176–80
colonialism 33, 36–7, 151, 154, 165
Cominform 42
Comintern 42
communication, means of 20, 62, 208
communism 41–2, 168, 175, 178–9, 185

Communist Party 34, 41–2, 125, 169, 173–8, 190
composite empire 13–14, 25–6, 30, 33, 101–20, 153
Congress of Vienna 133
conscription 29, 32, 34, 141, 166, 178, 207
conservatism 44, 130
Constantine the Great 113
Constantinople 12, 17, 20, 21, 24–5, 50, 55–6, 61, 86–7, 130, 132
constitutions 41, 137, 172–3, 193
Cossacks 30, 52, 70–71, 90, 94, 96–8, 106, 109–11, 113, 121, 123–4, 160
cotton 72, 151
Council of People's Commissars 169, 172–4
courts of law 87
Crimea(n Tatars) 14, 40, 45, 51–3, 58, 67, 70, 90, 107, 109, 115, 124, 133, 136, 139–40, 144, 186, 196–9, 201–4
Czechoslovakia 187, 191

Dagestan 132, *147*
Danelaw 61
Decembrists 22, 137
defensive line 70
dekulakization 36
democracy 22–4, 162, 199
Denikin, Anton 182
deportations 197
Diderot, Denis 126
diplomacy 74, 115, 130–31
Dmitrii Donskoi 84

Dmitrii Ioannovich 92–3, *93*, 95–6
Dn(i)epr (Dnipro) 61, 65, 110, 112, 198
Dolgorukii (Dolgorukov) clan 125
Don Cossacks 121
Don River 62, 198–9
Donbas 198–9
Donetsk region 198
dual faith (*dvoeverie*) 78
Duma (Imperial) 162
Dutch 25, 38, 46, 49–50, 71, 81, 88, 108, 110, 113–16, 128
dvor'iane (gentry) 99, 103
Dzerzhinskii, Feliks E. 160

early modern states 8, 30, 105–6
East Asia 15, 147
Eastern European Plain 7, 56, 59–60
Eastern Slavs 7–9, 12–13, 17, 20, 34, 49, 56, 59–7, 77–8, 80–81, 84, 90, 124, 196
education 36, 55, 128, 137, 141, 152–3, 157, 159, 172, 176, 200, 208
electricity 36, 178
Elizabeth I 26
Elizabeth II 11
Elizaveta Petrova 126–7
Emancipation Act (1861) *see* serfdom
English merchants 71, 88
Enlightenment 54–5, 57, 126, 130, 133
entrepreneurs 38, 136, 154
environment 202–3

epidemics 13, 36, 89, 93, 114
esotericism 24, 134
estate *see soslovie*
Estonia *see* Baltic region (states)
Eternal Peace (1686) 112
Eurasia 48, 66, 77, 121, 136, *149*
Euromaidan 201
European Union 200, 205

factories 37, 136, 151, 180
False Dmitriis 95–8
famines 13, 36, 93–4, 176–7, 179, 185–6
Fedotov, Georgii 78
Ferg(h)ana Valley 166
Ferry, Jules 82, 157
Filaret (F. N. Romanov) 98, 107–9
Filipp II 89
Filofei of Pskov 50, 87
Finland 118, 134, 156, 160, 166, 169
Finno-Ugrian 28, 56, 77, 124
Five Year Plans 45
Fletcher, Giles 57, 89
Fonvizin, Denis 129
foreign mercenaries 71, 109–10, 129
fossil fuels 75, 205
France 36, 38, 46–51, 54–6, 59, 61, 82, 107, 114–16, 128, 130–40, 145, 150, 154–8, 192, 209
Frederick II the Great 117
Frederick William I 117
French language 128, 157
French Revolution 126, 130, 137, 181

Friendship of the Peoples 28, 33, 175
furs (animal) 61, 71
Fyodor I 13, 57, 91–2
Fyodor II 96

gas (natural) 75, 203–5
gender *see* women
general secretary (of CPSU) 9, 173
Geok Tepe 150
Georgia 34, 45, 124–5, 131–2, 155, 170, 183, 196, 201
German 20, 25, 81, 124, 157
German speakers 82, 88–9, 127–8, 155, 186–7, 209
Germany 31, 59, 125, 136, 144–5, 152, 157–9, 162, 166–7, 186–7, 191, 204, 209
Germogen, Russian Orthodox Patriarch 98
glasnost' 193
Golden Age of Russian literature 129
Golden Horde (khanate) 70, 88
Golitsyn, Vasilii 115
Gorbachev, M.S. 192–4
Gorchakov, Aleksandr 151
Gosplan 41
government 7–8, 15, 22–6, 28–32, 41, 71, 75, 81, 95, 103–5, 112, 119–27, 130, 141, 145, 151–5, 160, 162, 168–9, 172, 178, 190, 194, 196, 205–8
Grand Duchy of Warsaw 132, 158
Grand Embassy of 1697–8 115–16
Great Britain 11, 14–15, 33–8, 40, 45–51, 61–3, 71, 75–6, 109, 114–16, 127–8, 133–6, 139–40, 145–6, 150–51, 154–5, 167–8, 187, 206, 209
Great Game 75–6, 146
Great Northern War 72
Great Powers (of Europe) 14, 23, 116–17
Great Reforms 32
Great Terror 36, 177, 179–80, 183–6
Great Turn 41
Great Wall (of China) 77
Greeks 17, 21, 55, 86, 133, 138
Greek Orthodoxy 17, 62, 86, 110, 138–9
Greek Project 55, 130
Grudzinska, Joanna 138
Gulag 29, 179, 185
gunpowder empires 183
Gustavus Adolphus, king of Sweden 108

Habsburgs 8, 135, 152, 162, 164, 183
Harpe, Frédéric-César de la 130
health care 36, 152
Henry VII 51
Herberstein, Sigismund von 57, 86
hetman 124
Hetmanate (Ukraine) 124
historiography *see* scholarship
Hitler, Adolf 15, 40, 42, 48, 125, 132, 181, 185, 189
Hittites 66
Holocaust 189
Holomodor 176, 185

239

Holy Roman Empire 8, 20, 47, 63, 109, 126
Hordes (*Orda*; Kazakh) 72
hostage-taking (*yasak*) 71
housing 104, 111, 202
Hungary 187, 191
Huns 59, 62, 66
hunting 28, 70–72

identity 8, 11, 17–37, 81–2, 95, 129, 138–9, 158–9, 178, 185–6, 208
ideology 7, 37, 50, 64, 126, 137, 139–40, 168, 174, 206; *see also* -isms
illiterates *see* literacy
Imperial Guards 118, 127, 137
imperial overstretch 15, 134
imperialism 36, 41, 45, 53, 71, 139, 146, 150, 154, 174–5, 177, 204
India 8, 14, 33, 135, 150–51, 183
industrialization 34, 36, 41, 72, 75, 135–6, 141, 144, 156, 159, 176, 189, 198, 203
Ingushetians 132, 166, 186
Inner Asia 40, 53
inoculation 36
inorodtsy 124
inovertsy 124
intelligentsia 81
Iran 8, 39, 54, 56, 75–6, 107, 132, 205
iron 72, 114, 119
Islam 29, 32–3, 48, 50–51, 67, 72, 77–8, 132, 147, 153, 160, 178, 184
Israel 189
Italy 87, 192

iurod' (holy fool) 94
Ivan I 83
Ivan III, the Great 13, 26, 49, 52, 56, 85–6, 90, 120
Ivan IV, the Terrible 10, 13, 26, 49–52, 57, 87–90, 92, 94–5, 98, 103
Ivangorod 108

Jadidism 33, 153
Jadviga, queen of Poland 84
Japan 15, 74–5, 133, 135, 144–7, 152, 167–8, 170, 204
Jesuits 95
Jews 55, 62, 159–60, 163, 189
John Casimir 82

Kalmyks 34, 121, 123, 186
Kamchatka 74
Kantemir, Antiokh 129
Karamzin, Nikolai 129–30, 134
Kashin *83*
Kazak(h)s 23, 28–9, 72, 75, 123–4, 134, 148–9, 160, 176–7, 185–6, 190
Kazan 51, 88
KGB 186
Khabarov, Erofei 74
Kharkiv (Kharkov) 198
Khazars 62
Khmel'nits'kii, Bohdan 31, 110–11
Khrushchev, Nikita 181, 190–91
Kim Il-Sung 189
Kipling, Rudyard 124–5
Kliuchevskii, V.O., 28, 36–7, 61
kniaz 63
Kol(')chak, Aleksandr 182

Komi 77, 195, 203
Konstantin Pavlovich 138
Korea(ns) 144–5, 179, 189
korenizatsiia 175–6
Kravchuk, Leonid 198–9
Kremlin (Moscow) 85, 98, 104, 169
Krizanich, Juraj 72
Krüdener, Julie de 134
Kuban region 176
kulaks 36
kulturnost' ('culturedness') 124–5
Kulturträger ('culture-bearers') 124, 152
Kurbskii, Andrei 89
Kyiv(an Rus') 7–8, 10–14, 27, 49, 56, 61–6, 77–8, 83, 88, 112, 137–8, 198, 201, 206
Kyrgyzstan (Kyrgyz; Kirghiz), 148

Lake Ladoga 63
Latin 20, 25–6, 86
Latvia *see* Baltic region (states)
legitimacy 15, 88, 112, 138
Lenin 11, 22, 36, 164, 166, 168, 175, 208
Leningrad 179, 188, 194
Lezgin 163
literacy 34, 128, 138, 141, 152, 208
Lithuania *see* Baltic region (states); Poland-Lithuania
Little (Mini) Ice Age 89
Livonia 51, 88
Livonian Wars 88–90, 108
Lomonosov, Mikhail 129
London 108, 115
Louis XI 51

Louis XIV 107, 208
Luhansk (Lugansk) region 198

Magyars 59, 62, 66
Manchuria(ns) 74, 144–6, 190
Mao Zedong 190–1
Marie Antoinette 130
marriage customs 92, 95–6
marriage politics 183
Marx, Karl 42, 152, 174–5, 182
Marxism-Leninism 41–2, 163, 174–5, 181, 184
Medvedev, Dmitrii 199
Mensheviks 179
merchants 99, 103
metropolitan 78, 89
'Middle Ground' 101, 107, 111, 121–3
Mikhail Romanov 46–52, 57, 98–9, 105–9
Military Revolution (early modern) 123
Miloslavskii, Ivan Mikhailovich 22
mining 72, 75, 114, 119, 203
Mniszech, Marina 96–7
modernization 33, 99, 113, 117, 130, 144, 176
Moldova 156, 169, 196
Molotov, Viacheslav 180
Molotov-Ribbentrop Pact 185
money, use of 103–4
Mongol(ian)s 9–13, 25, 27–8, 50, 56, 66–7, 76–80, 83–5, 88
Mongolia (region/state) 144, 170, 190
monks 50, 61, 77, 87, 98
Montesquieu 59

241

Mordovia 77, 195, 203
Moscow occupation 93, 97–8, 101, 132
Moscow rising of 1682 93
Moscow (State) University 129
Mughal emperors 107, 146
Mussolini, Benito 42

Napoléon I 40, 48, 131–2, 135, 158, 181
Narva 49, 108, 117
nationalism 15, 28, 31–4, 63, 82, 137–9, 152, 156–65, 169, 172, 174–9, 185–8, 191, 198, 202, 206, 208
navy 37, 54, 113, 115–16, *115*, 139, 144, 146, 183
Nazarbaev, Nursultan 23
Nazis 180, 186–8, 197
'near abroad' 34, 195
Nicholas I 11, 15, 125, 136–40
Nicholas II 34, 156–7, 160, 187
Nikon 110–13
Nobel brothers 151
nobility 57, 82, 97, 103, 125, 158
Nogais (Nogai Tatars) 107, 121
nomads 59–60, 62, 66, 121–2, 149
nomenklatura 173
Normandy 61
NATO 45, 183, 200–202, 205
Novgorod 40, 62, 79, 84–5, 87, 89–90, 200
Novikov, Nikolai 128, 130
nuclear weapons 16, 189, 205, 207
Nuremberg Trials 187

Oberprokuror 118
Ögödei 66
oil 75, 151, 203
Old Believers 111, 113
'opium of the people' 184
Opium War (First) 133, 135
oprichnina 89–90, 92
orda (Kazak polity) 123
oriental despotism 152
orthodoxy, autocracy, nationality 137–40
Ossetia (South) 201
Ottoman Empire 8, 17, 25, 39, 41, 49–52, 54–6, 87, 108–9, 114, 116, 118, 130–32, 135, 139, 144, 148, 152, 201

Pacific Ocean 40, 46, 67, 70, 74
paganism 62, 77–8, 84
palace coups 126–7
parliament (Russian) 162
patronage 130, 151
Paul I 126–7, 130, 137
peasants 14, 32, 81–3, 94, 101, 103–4, 131, 176, 178
Pechenegs 66
People's Commissar of Nationalities 165, 169, 175, 198
People's Commissar of War 181
People's Commissar of Internal Affairs, 224
perestroika 193
Peter, metropolitan 78
Peter I 10–11, 14, 22, 27–8, 30, 39, 54–8, 74, 85–7, 99–100, 108–9, 113–20, 125–8
Peter III, Russian tsar 126–7

Philosophical Letters (Chaadaev) 129
Pobedonostsev, Konstantin 160
Poland-Lithuania 40, 52, 55, 67, 84–6, 89-90, 96, 107–9, 111, 116–17, 132, 138, 151, 156, 158–62, 166–9, 191
Polish-Soviet War (of 1920–21) 169
Politburo 169, 173–4, 190
Polovtsy (Cumans) 66
pope (Catholic pontiff) 47, 52, 54, 95, 110
population numbers 35, 81–2, 88, 101, 103, 105, 138, 156–8, 176, 183–8, 190
Port Arthur 146
postal system 114
Potsdam Conference 187
Primary Chronicle 56, 61–3
printing 172
Pripet (Pripyat) marshes 59–60
proletariat (workers) 36, 164, 175–8, 208–9
propaganda 34, 140, 165, 168, 185, 208
Protestantism 49, 78, 96, 129, 159
Prussia 114, 117, 130, 135
Pskov 50, 79, 200
Pugachev, Emel'ian 121, 124
Pushkin, Aleksandr 129, 137
Putin, V. V. 9, 11, 16, 22–4, 28, 35, 45, 63, 99, 192, 199, 202–6

Qing Dynasty 39, 41, 74, 123, 144, 146, 183
Qipchaks 85

racism 124, 146
railroads 72, 75, 136, *145*, 151–2, 167, 174
rasputitsa 132
Razin, Stenka 70, 107, 113, 121
Riurikids 10, 13, 49–50, 63, 65
rivers 63, 65, 70, 85, 88, 113, 191 *see also* Volga
Romania 169, 187, 196
Romanov dynasty 10, 14, 49, 51, 56, 81, 89, 94, 98–9, 101, 104, 127, 146, 161–2, 164–5
Roosevelt, Franklin 187
rossiiskii 26, 81, 138, 152, 162, 195
rule of law 126, 187
Russian Federation 10–11, 16, 24, 26, 34–5, 44–5, 75, 120, 181–3, 195–206, 209
Russian language 9–10, 13, 26, 28, 61, 63, 67, 80–82, 87, 125, 128, 152–3, 157–8, 164–5, 177
Russian Orthodox Church 9, 12–13, 17, 21–2, 27–8, 32–3, 44, 49–53, 55, 62–3, 67, *73*, 75–8, 84, 86, 91–6, 98, 106, 110, 112, 129–30, 137–9, 178
Russification 158
russkii 81, 138, 152, 156–7, 195
Russo-Japanese War 133, 146–7, 152
Russo-Turkish War 144

Saakashvili, Mikheil 201
Safavid dynasty 39
St Petersburg 9, 15, 39, 45, 108, 117–19, 126, 130, 133, 137, 180, 194, 200
St Vladimir (Volodymyr) 8, 62

Sakhalin 204
Sarai 83
satellites 15, 107, 111, 132, 187, 189, 191, 193, 200
scholarship 10, 15, 24, 30, 39–40, 42, 45, 50, 57–8, 60, 82, 95, 106–7, 111, 134, 158, 172, 178, 202, 207–8
schools 37, 151–3, 172, 178, 196
science 74, 116, 118, 129, 185, 189
Scythians 66
Secretariat (CPSU Central Committee) 173
Security Council (UN) 192, 205
Senate (Russian) 22, 54, 118
serfdom 14, 32, 88, 94, 103–4, 110, 119, 140
service sector (of economy) 41
shah (Iranian ruler) 107
Shamil 147–8
shert' (treaty) 30–31, 111, 123
shipbuilding 113, *115*, 115–16, 119
Shuisky, Ivan 94
Siberia 14, 31, 37, 40–41, 49, 53, 56, 70–72, *73*, 74–5, 90, 105–7, 123–4, 134, 144, 148–50, 152, 156, 170, 179, 191, 204
Siberian exiles 137, 186
Sigismund Wasa, king of Poland 97–8
Silk Road 72
Skopin-Shuisky, Mikhail 97
slavery 22, 32, 58, 61, 90
Smolensk 52, 84, 86, 97
Smolensk War 51, 109

socialists 159–60, 162–3, 182
Socialist Revolutionaries (SR) 159
Sofia Paleologos 85–6
Sofia Vitovtovna 84
Solovetskii Island *29*
soslovye (estate) 119, 124, 141
sources, primary 28, 61, 101
South Korea *see* Korea
Soviet Empire 10–11, 14–16, *18–19*, 24, 30, 33–4, 37, 41–3, 46, 56, 58, 64, 76, 120, 125, 154, 164–70, 172–94, 196–201, 209
Soviet of Nationalities 172
Soviet nationality policy 33–4, 125, 162–5, 169–70, 172–80, 185–6, 193–4, 198–9
Spain 47, 132, 135, 207
Speranskii, Mikhail 31
Stalin 11, 22, 34–5, 41, 45, 74, 125, 163–5, 168–77, 180–81, 184–91, 197–9
standard of living 36–7, 104, 164, 192–3, 200, 207
State Committee for Emergency Situation 194
Stavropol region 176
steppe (grassland) 46, 59, 66, 121, *149*, 170
strel'tsy 30, 88, 100, 104, 106, 109, 118
Sudebnik (1497 Law Code) 85
Sumarokov, Aleksandr 129
Supreme Soviet 172
Sweden 39–40, 49, 52–4, 61, 97–8, 107–9, 114–18, 151, 201
Switzerland 130
szlachta 82, 103

Table of Ranks 119, 124–6, 154, 208
Taganrog 134
taiga 72
Tajikistan 29, 149, 166
Tatars 9, 11, 22, 26, 28, 31, 39–40, 50–55, 67, 70–71, 77–86, 88, 90, 107–9, 115, 121, 124, 160, 186, 197, 201, 203
Tatarstan 34, 195
taxes 104, 106, 144, 153
technology 20, 36, 75, 116, 135–6, 140–41, 150, 174, 176
Tehran Conference 187
terem 27
textile factories 72, 119, 151
theatre 145, 172, 189
Thirteen Years' War 53, 112
Time of Troubles 10–11, 13, 46, 49, 53, 70, 90, 92–105, 108–9
Tiraspol 196
Tolstoi, Lev N. 182, *182*
trade 32, 38, 51, 61, 65, 71–2, 74, 88, 90, 114, 116, 135
transport 20, 41, 62, 136, 174
Transsiberian Railroad 75
treaties (significant) 39, 55–6, 74, 111–12, 118–19, 131–2, 144, 166, 169–70, 185
triumphal entry into Moscow (1696) 55–6
Trotsky 168, 181
truces (significant) 51–3, 98–9, 112
tsar-batiushka 21, 113
Tukhachevskii, Mikhail 181
tundra 72
Turkestan *see* Central Asia

Turkic languages 80
Turkmenistan 72, 75, 148–50
Tver' 79, 83

Uglich *93*
Ukraine 10–17, 31–2, 34, 37, 40–41, 45, 49, 52–9, 61–5, 67, 70, 79, 81–2, 95, 104, 110–11, 124–5, 138, 156, 159, 163, 166–9, 176–7, 183–7, 190, 192, 196–205
Ukrainian 63, 67, 80–82, 125, 156–7, 177
Ulozhenie (1649) 30–31, 103, 110
Uniate Church 52, 95, 110
Union of Brest 52, 95
Union of Krewo 84
Union of Lublin 90
United Nations 192, 205
United States of America 16, 24, 38, 40, 45, 48, 133, 137, 144, 167, 187, 192, 200
universities 129, 131
Ural Mountains 40, 60, 66–7, 70, 72, 90, 114
urbanization 34, 164
Uvarov, Sergei 137–8
Uzbekistan 29, 34, 41, 66, 72, 148–9, 166
Uzhhorod 198

Varangians 56, 60–61, 63, 71
Vasily I 84–5
Vasily II 85
Vasily III 49, 57, 86–7
Vasily IV (Shuisky) 92, 96–8
velikii kniaz 20, 62
Vienna 114, 133–4, 158

245

Vietnam 192
Vladimir (town) 77–8, *79*, 79
Vladimir-Suzdal' region 62, 77
Vladivostok 144
voevody (governors) 30, 105–6
Volga 50–51, 62–3, 65, 67, 70, 83, 88, 107, 113, 121, 195
Volodymyr *see* St Vladimir
Voltaire 126–7
Vrangel, Pyotr 182

Warsaw 110, 132, 158
Warsaw Pact 42
water provision (supply) 36, 178
Western Europe 37, 53, 57–8, 61, 71, 78, 81, 109–10, 115–16, 118, 128, 192
Western merchants 71, 113–14
White Sea *29*, 46, 51, 88, 108
Whites (in Russian Civil War) 167–8
William III 116
Wladyslaw Jagiello (Jogaila) 84
Wladyslaw IV Wasa 98

women 27, 118, 138, 157, 169, *170*, *171*, 175, 191
wood *80*, 90, 104, 111
workers *see* proletariat
World War, First 15, 29–30, 162, 164–7, 175
World War, Second 36–7, 40, 112, 180–81, 188–9, 198

Xinjiang 190

Yanukovych, Viktor 201
Yalta Conference 187
yasak (fur tribute) 71
Yeltsin, Boris 195, 198–9
Yiddish 159
Yugoslavia 187, 192, 202
Yushchenko, Viktor 200–201

Zaporizhiya (Zaporozhe) 110, 124, 138
zemstvo 32, 36
Zhukov, Georgy 181
Zinov'ev, Grigorii 179, *179*